OLD D

10 *Easy Walks*

Gaynor Barton was born in Lancashire, England, and came to India in 1984 with her husband, a British Council officer, and their two children. An English teacher who has taught in Iran, Egypt and Brazil, Gaynor's interest in writing walks began in Worcester where she developed her first. She then went on to write more, related to the industrial archaeology of Scotland. During her husband's posting to Brazil she wrote a second guidebook, this time featuring the Portuguese colonial city of Olinda in Pernambuco. She now lives with her husband in Leicestershire and edits a local magazine.

Laurraine Malone was born in Sussex, England and came to India in 1982 where she spent five and a half years with her husband and their two children. As a secretary with the British Foreign Service, Laurraine worked in Botswana, Colombia, the former Soviet Union and Bahrain. Since leaving India she spent many years living in Dubai. An avid enthusiast of walking and exploring new places, she has also been developing her love for yoga—the latter influenced by her sojourn in India. Laurraine now lives with her husband in the UK.

OLD DELHI

10 *Easy Walks*

Gaynor Barton
Laurraine Malone

RUPA

Published by
Rupa Publications India Pvt. Ltd 1988, 2005, 2014
7/16, Ansari Road, Daryaganj
New Delhi 110002

Sales centres:
Allahabad Bengaluru Chennai
Hyderabad Jaipur Kathmandu
Kolkata Mumbai

Photographs by Gaynor Barton
Line Drawings by Gasparian
Maps by Uma Bhattacharya
Photographs on pages 17, 34, 150, 153 and 158 courtesy the British Library

ISBN: 978-81-291-3476-9

First impression 2014

10 9 8 7 6 5 4 3 2 1

The moral right of the authors has been asserted.

Printed at Gopsons Papers Ltd, Noida

For Alistair and Amber
Ben and Sam

Contents

Introduction to the Third Edition

In the mid 1980s Laurraine and I were friends, living in Delhi with our husbands and children and asked to do something for the British High Commission's 'Chrysanthemum Show'—a flower show and charity bazaar that was an important social event at the time. We wrote one walk; it was well-received and we were asked to write more.

We always enjoyed our visits to Old Delhi as the old walled city was so fascinating. In those days, as well as retail shops there were far more small workshops. Wandering the streets, you entered a past world as you could see books being printed on ancient presses, youngsters folding paper into envelopes, men making tiny components for the jewellery trade, others dyeing cloth or hammering designs into brass dishes. But many of these activities involved forges and were polluting, so the workshops were moved out. Good move, we thought. Cleaner air!

The Metro dominated the 2005 edition's update which took place in 2002. Kashmere Gate, Chawri Bazaar and Chandni Chowk Metro stations were all being built, creating tremendous upheaval on the roads and huge inconvenience to people living around the construction sites. But now they're up and running and Old Delhi's shopkeepers are thriving because of them. It was worth it!

But what's changed? The height of buildings has gone up! They used to be mostly two or three storeys, but now many are five storeys, and all the mosques and temples are expanding upwards—and outwards too if they possibly can. There's clearly more wealth around, as in the '80s poor children would latch onto any foreigner and pester them continually until they were given money. Now children do this far less. The inhabitants seem plumper and healthier than they were; the porters at Old Delhi Railway Station used to look very thin. Now most of them are strapping young men. Scooters have been replaced by motorbikes and, in fashion, saris by the salwar kameez. That was a surprise!

Of course, there's a downside. The higher buildings mean greater density of population, as well as the fact that all kinds of traffic—except tongas (horse-drawn carts)—have increased tremendously. The streets are infinitely more crowded too because of the millions brought in to shop by the Metro everyday; it's almost impossible to read a guidebook as you walk along now unless you get to Old Delhi early in the morning.

But in spite of the downsides, Old Delhi remains the most intriguing of places to explore. There's so much here that you can never be bored. For the more adventurous tourist or New Delhi resident, walking along at your own pace, with a guide book in hand, is still the best way of getting to know somewhere really well.

Useful Information

The Delhi Metro

At present there are three Metro stations in Old Delhi—all on the Yellow Line. They are Chawri Bazaar, Chandni Chowk and Kashmere Gate. However, in Phase Three of the Metro construction programme three more stations will be built. This line will link Mandi House with Kashmere Gate, while new Metro stations will be constructed at Delhi Gate, the Jama Masjid and the Red Fort. Work has already started and should be finished by 2016.

These new stations will help visitors reach Old Delhi much more comfortably than they do at present. The traffic jams on Netaji Subhash Marg everyday at peak times are horrendous, and being stuck in one, breathing in the fumes from hundreds of motorbikes and Autorickshaws, is most unpleasant. Try to avoid travelling to Old Delhi at peak travelling times—mornings between 8.30 a.m. and 11 a.m. and evenings between 5 p.m. and 7.30 p.m.

To use the Metro you can either buy a one trip token bought from the ticket desk or get a travel card, like a London Oyster Card, which you have to pay for initially but can use repeatedly and top up. With tokens you slide the token into a slot as you exit at your destination.

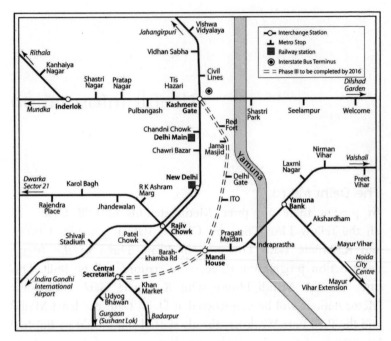

Delhi Metro Map

Buses

You can reach the Red Fort in Old Delhi very cheaply by bus. Amongst others, a number 246 will take you there. The bus stops at Shivaji Park, Zakir Husain College, Delhi Gate, Jama Masjid, Red Fort and Kashmere Gate before going on much further to terminate in Dilshad Garden. It's an orange-coloured Delhi transit bus. The best place to board to ensure you get a seat, is at the bus terminus itself, Shivaji Stadium—just off Baba Kharak Singh Marg. The bus station is easy to find as it is on the right just before you reach the State Emporiums, assuming you are walking away from Connaught Place.

Autorickshaws

Autorickshaw men never use their meters. They can give you a dozen excuses as to why they don't work although the main reason is, of course, because the fare shown is too little for their liking. It is essential to establish the price before entering and not to give in to any unfair price hiking at the end of the trip. Although the practice doesn't seem to be widespread, some of the Connaught Place Autorickshaw men are guilty of doing this.

Taxis

It's easy to phone for a taxi—you can pick up Delhi taxi cab numbers easily from a hotel or the internet—but it's hard to flag one down in the street. Unlike most European cities they don't circulate empty looking for passengers but return to designated taxi stands. Taxis have meters and they should be used, although often taxi drivers simply refuse to do so. In this situation you have to negotiate a price before getting in as you would in an Autorickshaw. There is a 25 per cent higher night rate which starts at 11 p.m. and ends at 5 a.m. The night rate does not start at 7 p.m.

Taxi drivers are notorious for bumping up fares for foreigners quite mercilessly, yet always with a winning smile, and know dozens of ways of achieving this end. The commonest is to take a contorted route to your destination or to rig the meter so that it runs very much faster than normal. Always try to find out roughly what the fare should be before getting into a taxi unless you've got money to burn.

Taking a Cycle Rickshaw

Old Delhi's cycle rickshaw men are invaluable for helping you get around and their prices are very reasonable. If you've lived here a while then you can probably get by with your basic Hindi but if you're new, or a tourist, and your destination is slightly off the beaten track it can be tricky. Many of Old Delhi's cycle and Autorickshaw wallahs do speak English, some very well. Others speak just enough to understand where you want to go. The English speaking fraternity congregate around the entrance to the Red Fort. You will undoubtedly pay more for hiring an English speaking rickshaw wallah but at least you won't waste precious time and end up in a strange street far from where you intended to go because your pronunciation of Khari Baoli sounded exactly like the name of an alley he knows in Daryaganj. You, of course, wanted the Fatehpuri Masjid area. The best advice is not to get into a scooter or cycle rickshaw unless you are absolutely sure he knows precisely where you want to go. If at all in doubt resist the 'Yes, yes, come on' of the men with a smattering of English and find someone else with whom you can have a short conversation.

If you have a simple destination such as Chandni Chowk, the Red Fort, the Spice Market, or the Jama Masjid then you don't need to find an English speaking rickshaw wallah. Unfortunately, rickshaw wallahs seem to hold the mistaken opinion that the faster they pedal the happier their passengers will be. Their most frequent boast is 'I am helicopter pilot'. Below are some useful phrases to help you settle a fare, give directions, and keep your 'helicopter pilot' grounded.

Kitne paise?	How much?
5	paanch
10	dus
15	pandrah
20	bis
25	pachis
30	tis
35	paintis
40	chaalis
45	paintaalis
50	panchaas

(Always settle the fare before climbing into the rickshaw.)

Giving Directions:

Seedhey	**Go straight ahead**
Daahiney	**Turn right**
Baayen	**Turn left**
Aur aagey	**Go a little further**
Ruk jaana	**Stop please**

Controlling the Speed:

Dheerey, dheerey	**Slowly, slowly**
Araam sey	**Take it easy/cool it**
Shukriyaa	**Thank you**

Shopping in Old Delhi

There are two large, quite distinct groups who shop here. Most of the smartly dressed men moving quickly from shop to shop along Old Delhi streets are shopkeepers themselves or agents of shopkeepers. Therefore, the character of Old Delhi trading is quite distinctive, as such an important segment of buyers aren't local people. These people have arrived by train at Old Delhi Railway Station and are staying in one of Old Delhi's many hotels and guest houses for a few days whilst doing business. They buy wholesale.

The second is the ordinary man or woman buying in single units for his/her own family's needs. This group has increased significantly since the arrival of the Chandni Chowk and Chawri Bazaar Metro Stations as so many more thousands of shoppers can get in to take advantage of the huge variety of goods and cheaper prices found in Old Delhi. The Metro is fast, cool, clean and you can travel 25 kms in forty-five minutes. It's a godsend if you live in Jahangir Puri or Green Park. You don't even need to change lines!

But if you do shop here, be careful. The shopkeepers are used to trading with knowledgeable, exacting customers and if you don't fall within this category they know instantly. There are no stringent consumer protection laws in India; it's very much a case of 'Buyer Beware'. Before you buy, check each product carefully, dismiss flattering remarks as sales-patter and be prepared to bargain.

Uniforms on the Streets of Old Delhi

There are always lots of policemen on the streets of Old Delhi. They wear khaki uniforms and carry guns as well as the long sticks called lathis—hence are often mistaken by foreigners for soldiers.

Soldiers wear dark green uniforms and green berets and are very much less common. Occasionally, you see blue uniformed soldiers belonging to a paramilitary force stationed at sites that may become flashpoints for inter-religious strife or other communal trouble.

Outlines of the Walks

Walk 1

The Red Fort—A walk around the lovely old buildings and gardens of Shah Jahan's palace fortress—the heart and soul of Mughal Delhi.

This walk can be taken on any day from dawn to dusk. Although the length of the walk is quite short, allocate at least two hours to it, as there's so much to be seen and appreciated.

Walk 2

Meena Bazaar—Sufi Shrines—the Jama Masjid—Firework Shops—Chawri Bazaar—Nai Sarak.

A magnificent mosque, fireworks, brass, books and saris. It's a good long walk for any weekday morning or Saturday morning. On Sundays many of the shops in the bazaars are closed, but if you only want to have a short walk limited to the Jama Masjid, then you could use this walk for any day, including Sundays.

Walk 3

The Digambara Jain Temple—The Jain Bird Hospital—Silver Street (Dariba Kalan)—Wedding Street(Kinari Bazaar)—The Jain Svetambara Temple—Ghantewala Sweet Shop.

This walk revolves around birds, bridegrooms and marble temples. Jain temples close from 12.00 p.m. to 5.00 p.m. every afternoon, so this walk is a good weekday morning or early evening walk. It should not be tried on a Sunday as the shops in Dariba Kalan and Kinari Bazaar are closed.

Walk 4

Turkman Gate—Holy Trinity Church—Dargah of Hazrat Shah Turkman Bayabani—Kalan Masjid—Sultan Razia's Tomb—Ajmeri Gate. If you have gained permission—The Madrasa and Tomb of Ghazi-uddin.

Ancient gateways, the Queen of Delhi's tomb and a pious seat of learning. This is a walk of contrasts, from bustling bazaars to quieter side lanes and can be taken at any time of the day. It is a good Sunday walk.

Walk 5

Kasturba Gandhi Marg—Poultry Sellers—Bazaar Matya Mahal—Chitli Qabar Bazaar—The Green Vegetable Market—Moti Mahal Restaurant.

This walk can be taken at any time of any day and is a good Sunday walk. If you wish to see the vegetable market at its busiest, start very early in the morning. (Matya Mahal is extremely busy so you need to be nimble to dodge the rickshaws.)

Walk 6

Khari Baoli Nuts and Spices Shops—The Spice Market (Gadodia)—The Fatehpuri Mosque—Haider Quli Khan's Gateway—Lala Chunna Mal's Haveli.

This walk is a chef's delight as it takes you to wholesale spice, pickle and preserved fruit shops. It's quite a short walk—an early morning weekday walk from about 9.30 a.m. In the afternoons and evenings this area is extremely busy. Gadodia, the wholesale spice market is closed on Sundays but many of the shops are open.

Walk 7

The Lajpat Rai Market—The Arya Samaj Building—Bhagirath Palace (Begum Samru's Palace)—Old Delhi Railway Station—The Sadhus of Bankhandi—Mahatma Gandhi Park—Old Delhi Town Hall.

Lost grandeur, sadhus and stations. This walk can be done

at any time of any day and is a possible Sunday walk if you are slim! (You need to squeeze between gates.) This is one of the longer walks.

Walk 8

The Garland Sellers —The Gauri Shankar Hindu Temple—The Sikh Sis Ganj Gurdwara—The Sunheri Mosque—The Dry Fountain (Bhai Mati Das Chowk)—The Bhai Mati Das Museum.

Garlands, temples, a gory tale and gory paintings in the museum. An early morning or late afternoon walk on any day. This is a good, short early morning walk. The Gauri Shankar temple closes at 11 a.m. and re-opens at 4 p.m.

Walk 9

The Lothian Road Cemetery—The British Magazine—The Telegraph Memorial—The Old Residency Building—St James' Church— Kashmere Gate.

An 1857 walk; where the British kept their gunpowder, fought long and hard and put memorials to their dead. A weekday walk for any time of any day as this area is quiet. It is a possible Sunday walk, although the Lothian Road Cemetery will definitely be closed and St James' Church will be holding services in the morning. (The Lothian Road Cemetery is sometimes closed on Saturdays too.)

Walk 10

Oberoi Maidens Hotel—The Civil Lines—Mother Teresa's Orphanage—The Park 'Qudsia Bagh'—The Nicholson Cemetery.

Places where members of the British Raj used to hold their parties, have their bungalows, play tennis and be buried. A gentle walk for any time of day and a good Sunday walk.

Walk 1:
The Red Fort

Opening Times

The Red Fort is said to be open from sunrise to sunset but in practical terms it is usually open from 9 a.m. to 6 p.m. Tuesday to Saturday. It's closed on Mondays.

Getting There

By Car

Park in the large, well-organized and well-known Red Fort car park in front of the fort's Delhi Gate. It is approached from Nishad Raj Marg. Charges vary according to length of stay but are always reasonable. It's open from 8 a.m. to 10 p.m. Then walk or take a cycle rickshaw to the main tourist entrance at Lahore Gate. It's a quiet, pleasant walk in front of the main west-facing curtain wall of the fort.

By Metro

At present the nearest station is Chandni Chowk but a new Red Fort station is planned in the Delhi Metro Phase 3 Development programme. This will make visiting the Red Fort delightfully hassle free.

The Red Fort

Begun in 1639 and completed in 1648, the Red Fort was built

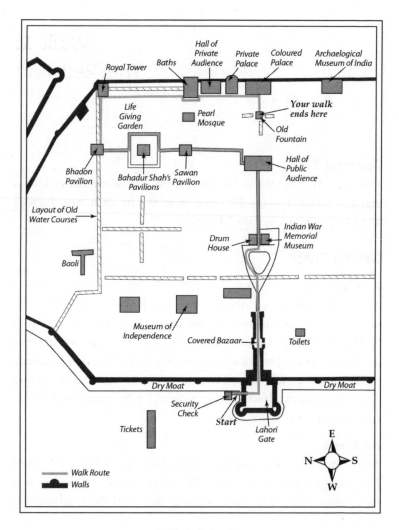

Walk 1: Route Map

at Shah Jahan's command. It was one of the two focuses of Shah Jahan's newly planned city of Shahjahanabad. The other one was the Jama Masjid, the large mosque near the Red Fort where Shah Jahan and his court used to pray. Shahjahanabad is now called Old Delhi.

The Walk

You enter the Red Fort by the Lahore Gate. Buy your ticket from the modern sunken ticket counter opposite the Lahore Gate. Keep it. You need to show it at the entrance to the Drum House (Naqqar Khana). A single ticket costs 250 rupees, 25 rupees for Indians. You can buy Sound and Light tickets here too and there are toilets nearby. There is a special ticket counter for foreigners, which means that even on very busy public holidays foreigners never need to queue for very long. Peer into the moat; you'll only see grass and cables today, but originally it was a considerable obstacle as it contained water to a depth of 30 ft., was crossed by drawbridges and stocked with fish. The fish are long gone— as the moat has been dry since 1857—but there used to be goats keeping the grass short. Unhappily, there was an accident involving two goats and an electric cable in which not only the goats but a man died too. The system of keeping the grass under control subsequently changed. Men with scythes do the work now.

The Lahore Gate

Cross the brick moat, built by the British after the Uprising (1857) to replace an old wooden one, and walk under the archway into the small courtyard behind. Once over the moat, you have to pass through security checks: a metal detector arch and brief body search—as at any Metro station. Men and women are treated separately with women checked behind a green privacy screen. Your bag will be put through an X-ray machine.

Stand in the courtyard with your back to the brick wall and

look at the magnificent gateway facing you. This was Shah Jahan's original west-facing Lahore Gate. The fortifications, on both sides and behind you, were added by Shah Jahan's son Aurangzeb. He built them to make it more difficult for an attacking army to enter the fort itself as the soldiers had to turn a full 90 degrees after penetrating the outer gate before even reaching the main gateway built by Shah Jahan.

As you stand facing the gateway you'll see two tall thin structures on your right. They look like Mughal lifts. They are lifts, but not Mughal. They have been built since the 1960s to take India's politicians to the top of the fortifications on 15 August, Indian Independence Day. Note the Indian flag flying in the breeze. During the British Raj the Union Jack was flown here. It was the burning ambition of many Independence Movement workers to lower the latter and hoist the former. That finally happened in 1947. There are two stone plaques on the left which tell you a little about how the fort has been used referring to the Uprising itself and the trials of INC (Indian National Congress) members held here.

Shah Jahan near the End of His Reign

Unfortunately, one sad consequence of the fort's continuing political importance is that for security reasons all the openings in Shah Jahan's gateway were blocked with red sandstone slabs in 1986. Turn round and look behind you. At the top of the lift, on the right, is a sandstone balcony with a white flagpole at its centre. On Independence Day, India's leaders are seated on either side of the flagpole and in rows in front of it. It is now impossible for a sniper to fire at them from Shah Jahan's gateway, but the gateway itself has been blinded.

Walk towards the gateway and inspect the huge bronze-covered wooden door on the left which is the original. The one on the right is missing, as it was destroyed by the British when they attacked the fort in 1857. Take a look at the thickness of the door and consider its weight. It's said elephants were used to help open and close doors like these.

Chatta Chowk (The Covered Bazaar)

Enter Chatta Chowk. Bazaars in seventeenth century India were normally in the open air. A covered bazaar was extremely unusual and this one was quite exceptional. It was based on one in Persia.

Once inside the gateway you see that shops on the right such as Virender Art Emporium and Famous Maharaja Art Palace have taken over areas that used to be used by guards. Opposite these shops you can see the guard rooms as they were. Walk a little further in, stand on the left and look across to Shop No. 19, The Treasure House. Above the shop's modern sign you can see the top of the original cusped arch of one of Shah Jahan's shops. Each shop on the lower arcade must have had an arch like this.

In Shah Jahan's time, there were shops on both the upper and lower levels and you can clearly see the shape of Shah Jahan's original arches—although, except for a small window, most of the archway has been filled in. In the recent past, families used to live here above the shops, only the army moved them out for security reasons. Today, the upper level has an abandoned, neglected air about it and it's hard to imagine these upper arches filled with beautiful women showering petals on imperial processions passing beneath. Today, the shops specialize in souvenirs—300 years ago they catered to the luxury trade of the imperial household as they specialized in silks, brocades, velvets, gold and silver ware, jewellery, and gems. There were coffee shops too where nobles sat discussing the latest campaigns, successes and defeats, of Mughal armies.

Walk to the middle of the bazaar where there's an open section to let in light and air. Around and above you, the sandstone has been covered in whitewash as nowadays Chatta Chowk is given a facelift once a year just before Independence Day. A coat of white paint wasn't Shah Jahan's style, however. In his time the natural sandstone was covered with beautiful paintings.

There is a modern toilet block near here. Look for the green TOILET sign on the right. The charges vary from 2 rupees to 5 rupees.

Walk to the end of the Chatta Chowk shop area and pause on the left-hand side just after you've left the shade of the covered bazaar. Consider the view ahead. There are Victorian British barracks on the left, trees, and a circular lawn. In Shah Jahan's time none of this existed. The view of the Drum House (a music gallery above a gateway) from this spot used to be excellent, as there was nothing in front of it except a large square courtyard containing a water tank. The square was surrounded by single-storeyed arcaded rooms used by Mughal officials, commanders, and ministers who needed to be near the Hall of Public Audience just behind the Drum House. (Consult your sketch map on page 2.) Then look behind you on your left and focus on the brown brickwork just beneath the red sandstone crenulations. You can see set within it the arches of homes constructed by Shah Jahan's builders for the imperial servants and their families, which were the width of the wall. The small dwellings at ground level are modern. Keeping to the left, walk towards the cross roads where the road from Chatta Chowk meets a main north-south running road and decide what you want to do. If you wish to visit either the Freedom Struggle Museum or the Baoli turn left.

Walk
1
ॐ☉ॐ

The Museum of Independence (The Swatamtreta Sangram Sanghralaya) and the Baoli

It's signposted to the 'Museum of Independence' and well worth visiting if you are interested in the long struggle to gain independence from the British. On the ground floor there are many dramatic paintings illustrating military battles in the Uprising of 1857 as well as some of the horrors meted out by the British—such as being tied to a cannon's mouth! On upper levels in the museum, there can be found a mass of information on all the main characters of the freedom struggle, such as Subhash Chandra Bose and Mohandas Gandhi as well as descriptions of crucial events such as the Bonfire of Foreign Clothes and the Salt March. The dioramas, however, leave much to be desired.

The Baoli (A Stepped Well)

For anyone who has never seen a stepped well here's an opportunity to make good the deficit. To find it, keep walking away from the Museum of Independence. You'll come to the stepped well on your right—there's an explanatory stone in front of it. However you can't walk down the steps of the stepped well; it's not open to visitors. You simply have to content yourself with looking at it from the path.

The North-South Running Road

If you decide not to turn left, consider the north–south running road ahead of you for a moment. This road was important in Shah Jahan's time because there were hundreds of small rooms used as workshops, offices, and storerooms on either side. It was here that craftsmen such as carpet weavers, jewellers, tailors, gold and silver smiths were found, as also the astrologers, poets, military record keepers, and the inevitable tax collectors. There were sheds too for elephants, camels, horses and cows at its most northerly end. Even the Royal Mint was along this long, north-south running road. All have gone. The British authorities demolished an estimated

80 per cent of the Red Fort's buildings after taking over in 1857.

Walk towards the red sandstone Drum House where your ticket will be checked. Look at it from a distance before you pass through.

Naqqar Khana (The Drum House)

This solid structure was once an important gatehouse with a music gallery above. In Mughal times the music could float out from under the cusped arches; the wooden frames and glass you see there now are nineteenth century additions.

The instruments were large kettle drums, hautboys (shehnai—a kind of oboe), and cymbals. The musicians played during the emperor's morning meetings in the Hall of Public Audience, to indicate prayer times, imperial or diplomatic comings and goings, and to celebrate festivities both religious and domestic, such as birthdays.

In seventeenth century India it must have been quite easy for a respectable local person, with a reason to be inside the walls, to enter the Red Fort and reach the Drum House—but from this point onwards it got more and more difficult. The palaces along the river front were absolutely impenetrable. From the Drum House all but royal princes had to dismount and, like you, walk on.

Shah Jahan believed that lilies could be gilded. Walk to the facade of the Drum House facing the Hall of Public Audience; then turn around and look above you to one side of the arch itself. All the flowers, stems, and leaves were once of gold, standing out against the redness of the sandstone. Thus Shah Jahan, from his canopied throne in the building ahead of you, looked onto a magnificent facade. A blank red wall just wasn't good enough for him.

Walk straight ahead to the Hall of Public Audience along a path dividing a lawn. Climb the steps and enter the Diwan-i–Am.

Walk
1
ೞೕೞ

Diwan-i-Am (The Hall of Public Audience)

Now that most of its finery has gone, this pavilion has an elegant, bare red beauty. But it used to be so different. 300 years ago this hall didn't even look red as all the sandstone was hidden behind a very thin layer of white plaster which was polished to shine like white marble. These white walls were decorated with gold stucco work and were in perfect harmony with the colour of the marble throne.

Look at the marks on the red sandstone pillars in front of the marble throne canopy. At one time there was a gold-plated railing surrounding the canopy which marked off an area from the rest of the hall within which stood the princes and great nobles. Besides the gold one, there was a silver railing within which the lesser nobles stood. The marble platform in front of the throne canopy was used by the prime minister (wazir), who stood on it to pass petitions to the seated emperor.

In front of the hall was a courtyard, stretching to the Drum House—not the lawns you see today. This courtyard was covered by a beautiful canopy held up by massive silver-plated poles. There was a third railing made of red sandstone in the courtyard. Its use was to divide minor officials from the crowd who had simply come to stand and stare. The canopy above them could shade 1,000 people.

Beneath your feet today are flagstones, but in Shah Jahan's time the floor was covered with silk carpets. Heavy curtains hung from the outside of the building and you can still see the curtain and canopy rings if you look above the pillars on the exterior walls. These, however, are not Shah Jahan's; his were copper. These curtains were raised and lowered by a system of ropes.

Walk over to the marble throne canopy. It is known as 'The Seat of the Shadow of God'. It is said that no matter where you stood in this hall, you could see the emperor on his throne and he could see you. He was glitteringly prominent in splendid clothing, bedecked with pearls and precious gems. Shah Jahan used to spend about two hours a day here between 8 and 10 in the morning. He worked on the routine matters of government; choosing people for posts, receiving military reports, reading letters from provincial governors and citizens, and settling disputes. On Wednesdays, justice was meted out from here, or from another building, the Adalat Khana. The emperor's hangmen, with their axes and whips, would be nearby so that the sentences could be carried out promptly.

Look at the inlaid panels behind the throne canopy: it is assumed that they were made in Florence by Austin de Bordeux, but all the intervening intricate floral inlay work was done by Indian craftsmen. The small central figure at the top, in an arched inlay in the middle, above a square inlay of a cock with a fancy tail, is of Orpheus, the legendary Greek hero, who was such a wonderful musician he could make trees and even rocks follow his singing. Figurative workmanship is very unusual in Islamic buildings and this one panel is the only example in the whole of the Red Fort. This, however, is very hard to see.

Stand facing the throne canopy and walk a few steps to your right, so as to look up at the ornate red sandstone window in the wall in front of you. The emperors' daughters used to sit behind this screen listening to all that was taking place while remaining invisible to view.

With your back to the Drum House, leave the Diwan-i-Am by the steps on its left. Once on the path, walk forward for a few paces and then turn left, aiming for the wall you can see at the end of the path. At present it is red. This is actually the rear wall of the pavilion marked on your map as Sawan, which in turn is one of a pair of identical pavilions in the Hayat Baksh Garden. Stop on the path next to the Sawan pavilion.

Hayat Baksh Bagh (The Life-giving Garden)

From the Sawan pavilion you can see the other pavilion in the distance; that one's called Bhadon. These names reveal the whole character of this life-giving garden as they refer to the monsoon

Walk
1

months in India. Sawan is the first month of the rainy season (July) and Bhadon the second (August). This garden used to be so alive with water and fountains that it created the effect of monsoon showers. Nobles would sit in the pavilions to admire the gardens.

Look at the back wall of the Sawan pavilion; this is where water freely flowed from. There is a slit just above the marble shelf and you will be able to see the niches in the wall beneath. Water cascaded through the slit over the niches which contained gold and silver pots of flowers. At night, the niches held lighted candles. Water flowed from this pavilion along a channel to a square pool in the centre of the garden. The pool area is now empty and there's a red sandstone pavilion in the centre which was built in the nineteenth century by a doomed Mughal descendant! In Shah Jahan's time there was a pavilion here too, but you couldn't see it clearly as it was almost hidden by the jets of water from the 281 fountains surrounding it. There were forty-nine around the pavilion itself, 112 lining the tank and thirty in each of the four channels flowing towards the central tank. Shah Jahan's pavilion may possibly have been marble. Today, you can see three red sandstone bases of fountains in each channel where formerly there were ten times as many silver-plated ones.

Walk towards the marble pavilion named Bhadon—and as you cross the red sandstone pavilion between the two (Sawan and Bhadon), spare it a glance. Its builder was doomed—seeing as he was the last Mughal king, Bahadur Shah Zafar, who ended his days as a prisoner of the British in Rangoon. In happier times he would sit in this pavilion, surrounded by water, listening to poets read their works to him and contributing by reading his own poems aloud to them. Bridges linked the pavilion to the surrounding paths. The areas which are lawns today were formal Persian style gardens in Shah Jahan's time filled with fruit trees and flowers and divided by running water and fountains. Contemporary descriptions of this garden talk of their 'tangled branches cutting out the sun'. This garden must have been very beautiful indeed.

Once you've reached the second marble pavilion you'll see that here again vases of flowers or lighted candles would be placed in niches to allow water to tumble over them. White marble is now the dominant building material and it was brought from mines near Jaipur or from Gujarat. (The sandstone came from mines near Agra.)

The path turns 90 degrees and you'll find yourself walking towards a white marble building ahead of you with a taller structure poking up behind it.

Shahi Burj (The Royal Tower)

The tower, made of sandstone but now partly painted white, is closed to the public as it was seriously damaged during the fighting of 1857 and is still unsafe. There's a white marble pavilion in front of it, but it is the tower behind that is the original Shahi Burj. This tower had three storeys of which the lower storey contained a water tank into which water was raised by a waterwheel from the river Yamuna. From here it flowed into the canal known as the Stream of Paradise (Nahr-i-Bihist) and began its journey along the royal terrace. Today, you can't see the river Yamuna at all. Yet it used to be so close that in 1784 a prince, worried about losing his royal life, jumped from the royal tower into the river, swam across it and fled to Lucknow. Shah Jahan used the upper rooms of this tower as his most private working place. Only his sons and three or four senior officials were allowed here, to discuss matters of state with him.

There is some disagreement about who built the white marble pavilion in front of the Shahi Burj. Was it one of Shah Jahan's last designs or was it built by his son Aurangzeb? It was certainly built later than the tower. Water used to run down the marble chute at the back of this marble pavilion to create a background noise in order to make eavesdropping on royal conversations more difficult.

You cannot enter the pavilion. Instead, walk a little distance away and look at the roof above. The shape of this roof is one of the hallmarks of Mughal architecture as it imitates, in marble, the thatched roof of a seventeenth century Bengali dwelling.

Before leaving this pavilion look along the length of the royal terrace. Imagine the route of the Stream of Paradise flowing south to the building in the distance which contained the royal baths. Behind the baths are the domes of the most magnificent building in the Red Fort: the Hall of Private Audience. The domes were (of course) gilded.

Walk along the path towards the baths. You'll pass a small nineteenth century white marble pavilion on the terrace on your left which looks bare and isolated without occupants or a Paradise Stream flowing past.

The baths are closed. If you walk around the building you can stand on a stone bench and peer through a window for a glimpse of the marble-inlaid floors and columns. There were hot steam baths, cold baths and, most luxurious of all—a fountain scented with rosewater in a dressing room. On the wall of the baths opposite the entrance to the Moti Masjid, at ground level, are the outlines of two large squares. These squares were once openings through which wood was fed into fires to heat the royal bathwater.

The building opposite the baths is the Moti Masjid. It's closed to the public.

The Moti Masjid (Pearl Mosque)
This mosque was built by Aurangzeb, Shah Jahan's son. Some argue that he built it because he felt less secure than his father and didn't like crossing to the Jama Masjid outside the Red Fort's walls, or perhaps more simply, as a devout Muslim, he felt the Red Fort needed a mosque. It took five years to build and cost 1,60,000 rupees—a fortune at the time. An interesting architectural feature is that the outer red sandstone walls, aligned with the

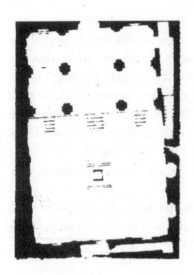

Plan of the Moti Masjid

other buildings in the Red Fort, get further away from the inner marble structure of the mosque itself which is aligned with Mecca. Look at the plan. By constructing the mosque in this way Aurangezeb's Moti Masjid didn't spoil the symmetry of the palace buildings. It fits in perfectly. The domes used to be covered with copper—so it couldn't have been the domes that gave the mosque its name. A pearl is small, white and exquisite and Aurangzeb must

Walk
1
෯◉◠◑෯

have thought his mosque was too.

Walk to the Diwan-i-Khas now, the next building along from the baths on the royal terrace.

Diwan-i-Khas (The Hall of Private Audience)

There's a very famous inscription in this room but it's tricky to see. If the hall is roped off and you'd like to find the text—this is where to go: walk down from the royal terrace and stand on the path more or less parallel to the centre of the hall. Then, more precisely, face the marble pediment that used to be a throne base and position yourself next to the third pillar from the left of the outer set of arches. Look at the three cusped inner arches on your right and note that above the smaller arch to the right of the slightly larger central arch you can just see Persian script ornately enclosed by tendrils and flowers. As the script is very ornate and unfamiliar to Western eyes and this upper area above the columns is in shadow, it is very difficult to make out. It says: 'If there is a Paradise on earth'; look, now, across to the left of the central arch for the couplet's completion: 'It is here, it is here, it is here.' (You read Persian like Arabic, from right to left not left to right.) It was composed by the poet Amir Khusrow.

The same couplet is repeated above the right and left-hand arches of the opposite wall. Paradise is no longer here, as this hall, which was sumptuous beyond belief, has gone through difficult times.

Flowers Made from Semi-precious Stones in the Diwan-i-Khas

Yet a hint of its glory remains. Specialists have carefully cleaned the marble and replaced some of the precious stones prised out by the many different groups of foreign soldiers billeted in the fort, as well as home-grown vandals. Look at the first row of pillars at the front of the hall. Study the inlay work of one of the larger flowers in the centre of a panel springing from the base of the column. The stones are: lapis lazuli for the blue of the centre; jasper for the small mustard yellow petals; agate and carnelian for the outer red ones; jade for all the green stems and leaves; and mother-of-pearl for the very fine veins of the leaves.

Walk
1
৯⊙৵⊙৯

To give an indication of the original splendour of this magnificent hall, a small section of one column has been re-gilded. To see it, walk up the steps to the right of the Diwan-i-Khas onto the terrace and then turn to face the Diwan-i-Khas itself. A little of the upper section of the second column of an inner arch has been re-gilded.

As with the earlier hall you visited (Public Audience), here too your imagination has to add things: beautiful carpets, rich brocade hangings, curtains, a ceiling decorated with sheets of gold, and a throne so splendid it sent a French jeweller of the time into a long ecstasy of descriptive delight. The Peacock Throne was about 6 ft. long and 4 ft. wide, a little like a single bed on sturdy gold gem-studded legs. From the base of the 'bed' sprang twelve gold gem-studded columns supporting a gold canopy lined with diamonds and pearls and fringed with pearls. It was on top of this canopy that the peacock stood displaying its sapphire-studded tail. On either side of the peacock was a large bunch of gold flowers inlaid with precious stones. It was estimated to have cost 10 billion rupees in the 1630s. It was Shah Jahan's best throne. (He had six others.) Matters of state were debated and fully discussed in this hall. Formal proclamations were made in the other one (Public Audience) but policies were argued out by the emperor in consultation with his senior ministers here. It was the Mughal equivalent of the Cabinet Secretariat in Rashtrapati Bhavan, or Britain's No. 10 Downing Street.

The View from the Royal Terrace

Walk
1

Stay on the royal terrace and look over the other side at the lawns and the Ring Road. The view from this wall is an attractive one these days. Beneath is a pleasant park while across the busy Ring Road are the green lawns and trees surrounding the cremation sites of some of India's national leaders: Mahatma Gandhi, Jawaharlal Nehru, Lal Bahadur Shastri, Indira Gandhi and her sons Rajiv and Sanjay. In many ways, this area carries out one of the functions of Westminster Abbey; if not a final resting place there's the memory of a final fire. This situation is important to Hindus as the sacred river Yamuna is near here and an extremely old public cremation ground is just to the north at Nigambodh Ghat. Leave the royal terrace by walking down the steps and walk left along the path. Look for the archway on your left which has a few steps beneath it going down to a large gate at the bottom.

Take a look at this gate.

The Water Gate (Khizri Gate)

It has a forgotten air about it now, but this gate was an important

View of the City of Delhi, from the River Jumna.
London, Published 20 August 1857

entrance for the emperor himself and his most senior nobles. Shah
Jahan first entered his new fort through this gate, as he thought it
auspicious because it faced Mecca. Its alignment certainly didn't
bring luck to the last occupant of the Mughal throne. He fled
through it in 1857, only to be quickly captured and later tried
by the British here in his own palace. Throughout its life, this
entrance was convenient for bringing people into the Red Fort
quietly as they could sail up the river, beach on the sandy shore
and then enter through this gate.

From the archway of this river gate, continue walking straight
ahead and walk up the ramp to the royal terrace again. The
building above this gate is the Khas Mahal, or the Private Palace.

Khas Mahal (The Private Palace)

Turn to face the Khas Mahal and to your right you'll see a marble
balcony overhanging what is now a park but used to be the river
bank. Imagine that it's 1652, that it's sunrise and that beneath
you on the bank between the fort wall and the river is a crowd
of people. You're the emperor and the people have come to see
you, to reassure themselves that all is well and perhaps tell you

their complaints. If an emperor didn't make his daily appearance here, there was near panic in the city. The illness or death of an emperor meant that troubled times lay ahead, as sons squabbled and fought for the empty throne.

The room leading into this Balcony of Audience was the emperor's private sitting room. Across the Stream of Paradise was his bedroom and off that, a small prayer room. Shah Jahan was in bed by 10 p.m. after working a twelve-hour day. Look at the beauty of the marble screen over the water channel. It is undoubtedly the best filigree work in the Red Fort.

Look up at the 'Scales of Justice' above the filigree grill. If you're standing with your back to the Coloured Palace (Rang Mahal) you'll see moons surrounding the scales. If your back is to the Diwan-i-Khas you'll see a host of circulating suns. The sun is frequently used to symbolize Mughal royalty. It's most appropriate for suns to be here as this side faced the throne of the 'sun' himself: the emperor.

Walk to the next building.

Walk
1
ॐ⊙ॐ

Rang Mahal (The Coloured Palace)

This was a royal ladies' common room and the place where the emperor ate most of his meals. During meal times the much prized carpets were protected by stitched-together leather sheets which in turn were covered by calico cloths. You can't enter this building either so you have to admire the glittery veins criss-crossing the ceiling from the terrace itself. It's said these rooms look particularly beautiful when lit by candles at night, as the mirrors reflect thousands of tiny flames. These rooms are called Sheesh Mahal or the Hall of Mirrors.

The Rang Mahal itself was a beautiful hall. The ceiling above was silver, decorated with golden flowers which reflected in the water of the channel and the lotus pool beneath.

But although it was very beautiful, sometimes the ladies got bored. There is said to have been an eighteenth century woman, the empress of Jahandar Shah, who sat gazing out at the river one day and remarked that she'd never seen a boat sink. Very shortly afterwards, a boat was capsized so that she could be entertained by watching the people bobbing about and listening to their cries for help before they drowned.

In summer the ladies went underground. The rooms aren't open to visitors but you can see the grills that allowed air into them. Walk down the steps at the far end of the hall and look beneath floor level at the red sandstone ventilation screens. If you kneel down and peer through the screens you can see the tops of vaulted arches. These underground rooms would have been cool not just because they were cellars but because the water channel flowed above them. They were beautifully decorated. It's said that these rooms could be as much as 10 degrees cooler than the ones above.

Turn to face the marble fountain.

The Marble Fountain

Entertaining and impressing foreign dignitaries was an extremely important aspect of the Mughal imperial court, and around this fountain is where the emperor displayed the richness and sophistication of Mughal culture. Sadly, today it looks a little like a large empty paddling pool! Shah Jahan, his closest men friends and allies, would watch from the balcony you can see in the red sandstone building facing you, whilst the women watched from the Rang Mahal behind you. Remove the ugly white concrete block which surrounds the marble fountain today and replace it with a far more delicate marble structure, add water to the pool and place dancing girls, musicians, storytellers and poets around it. Hang elegant lights around the pool and imagine them shimmering in the water. Guests would be seated on beautiful carpets. The area was transformed into one of stunning beauty and the entertainments held here were said to be absolutely magnificent.

Your walk ends here. However, if you have extra time then visit the Archaeological Society of India Museum which is the next building along on the royal terrace. The contents are of a wide range: they include miniature paintings, calligraphy, stone carvings, chess sets, Chinese porcelain, astrolabes and even examples of late Mughal clothing. The lighting, however, is poor and the method of display unimaginative.

Shah Jahan: A Few Background Notes

Shah Jahan means 'Emperor of the World'. It was a title given to him by his father Jahangir whose own title meant 'Seizer of the World'. Shah Jahan received this title after political success in the Deccan, at a time when he still went by his own name, Khurram. The title 'Shah Jahan' in itself is magnificently grand. It never of course came near to reflecting reality; although it is possible that in those seventeenth century days, Shah Jahan, as emperor, was the richest king in the world. He was undoubtedly one of seventeenth century's greatest architects. Shah Jahan decided to move his capital to Delhi from Agra in 1638. He was forty-six years old at the time and had ruled the empire of Hindustan for ten years. His father Jahangir had died a natural death, but to ensure his own succession Shah Jahan had ordered the deaths of his brother, two nephews and two male cousins. Mumtaz Mahal, Shah Jahan's favourite wife, had died several years earlier after bearing him fourteen children, and he was building her beautiful mausoleum, later known to the world as the Taj Mahal, in Agra. In 1638 it was far from finished but Shah Jahan, who loved buildings, was dissatisfied with Agra as a capital city.

He wanted to build a city which would not only outshine Agra, the city built by his grandfather Akbar, but also rival that newly-planned and dazzling Persian capital he'd heard so much about—Isfahan. He wanted to leave his mark on the world. He also found Agra too hot, coupled with the fact that the streets were so congested that he couldn't hold the splendid processions he loved. So he decided to move.

By 1638, Shah Jahan was an experienced builder. He'd had over thirty years of involvement with architectural matters as he'd redesigned his own living quarters in Kabul when he was only fifteen and changed buildings erected by his grandfather and father to suit his own taste. In Agra, he built Akbar's red sandstone palaces in marble and in Lahore, pulled down Jahangir's Hall of Private Audience and built another one. His city in Delhi he named Shahjahanabad and his palace, Quila-i-Mubarak—the Auspicious Fort. (Its present name, the Red Fort, dates from the days of the British Raj.)

After the completion of the palace fortress in 1648, Shah Jahan only spent nine years ruling from within it before deciding to hand over to his favourite son and retire to the older palace fortress in Agra.

Shah Jahan's plans went astray. The son he'd hoped would rule was outwitted, out-fought, and finally murdered by another of his sons, Aurangzeb. Shah Jahan's retirement became imprisonment in the same fort in Agra in which he'd designed the marble palaces at the beginning of his reign.

Walk
1
ॐ✶ॐ

Walk 2:
The Jama Masjid

A magnificent mosque, brass, wedding invitations, books and saris. This is a walk packed with people and specialist bazaars. It's a good walk for early mornings on weekdays, bearing in mind that the mosque will be closed for longer periods of time on a Friday. In the past, most of the bazaars closed on Sundays, but nowadays many of the shops themselves stay open. To add to the commercial intensity of trading there's also a huge and hectic Sunday Market held on the pavement of Subhash Chandra Bose Marg every Sunday, which has expanded into all the nearby streets. If you don't like crowds don't attempt this walk on a Sunday. Local people, especially young men, who are working during the week, flock here to find bargains.

General Information about the Jama Masjid
The Jama Masjid can change its nature rapidly—from being the focus of intense Islamic belief for thousands of Muslims, to that of a commercialized tourist hotspot where large numbers of foreign visitors tipped out of tourist buses are efficiently processed. Be prepared for change. Every visit you make to the Jama Masjid will offer a different experience.

If you choose to visit the Jama Masjid in the afternoons you may find the mosque closed for prayers. Prayer times vary between summer and winter, Fridays and weekdays and festival times.

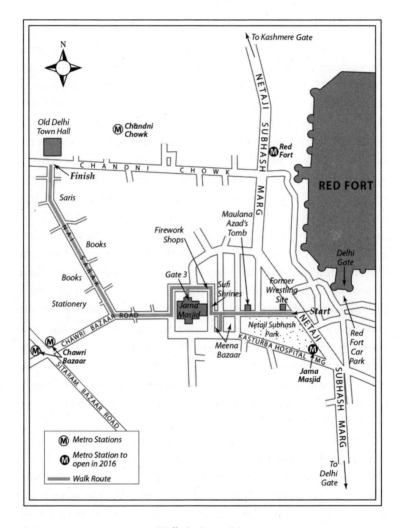

Walk 2: Route Map

As a rule of thumb, however, the best times to visit are:

8.30 a.m.	to	12.00 p.m.
2 p.m.	to	3.30 p.m.
4.30 p.m.	to	5.30 p.m.

To many visitors, one of the highlights of the visit is climbing the minaret and taking photographs from the top. On clear days the view is spectacular. Please remember the minaret closes at sunset, which is usually about 5.30 p.m., but bear in mind you can't climb up during prayer times, and the man in charge at the bottom gives you little time on top if you begin the ascent near to a prayer time. In the past there was a strict rule that a woman on her own couldn't climb the minaret. Nowadays this ruling has become more of a grey area, especially as the charge for taking a camera into the mosque (300 rupees in 2014) includes the cost of climbing the minaret. Certainly the mosque authorities prefer women to climb the minaret with someone else as they say they are concerned about one woman alone becoming dizzy. Surprisingly, they are not concerned about the dizziness of lone men. Climbing alone is now a 'Health and Safety' issue. If you are a woman on your own tag onto someone else's party, or you could ask the young man at the base of the minaret—the 'minaret guide'—to climb with you. He'll tell you a little about the mosque from the platform at the top and expect 100 rupees as a tip when he returns you safely to the bottom.

Don't even consider climbing the minaret if you are unfit, claustrophobic or unhappy in the dark. Natural light does enter in places but many of the early steps are made in complete darkness. There are no electric lights in the minaret. People ascend and descend at the same time which can be a squash if two large bodies meet in the middle. These days the general rule is that people coming down the minaret squash themselves onto the outer wall of the staircase and those ascending squash themselves against the inner. However, not everyone knows this! The passage is a narrow one.

Places of Interest
MEENA BAZAAR
SUFI SHRINES
THE JAMA MASJID
FIREWORK SHOPS
CHAWRI BAZAAR
NAI SARAK

Getting There

By Car
Park in the large, well-organized and well-known Red Fort car park in front of the fort's Delhi Gate. It's approached from Nishad Raj Marg. Charges vary according to length of stay but are always reasonable. Then, take a scooter or cycle rickshaw to the Jama Masjid. Tell the driver you want the Jama Masjid Meena Bazaar Gate. (Consult your route map). Or you can walk to the Jama Masjid from your car as it isn't far. With your back to the car park, turn left onto Nishad Raj Marg, and then at the junction of Netaji Subhash Marg, turn right. Cross the road and after walking for about five minutes you'll reach the Meena Bazaar Gate on your left. The approach to the Jama Masjid is lined on both sides and down the centre with stalls selling a myriad of goods: jeans, children's clothing, shoes, blankets, waterproof watches, toys, mirrors and prayer mats. If you are taking this walk before the feast of Eid Al-Adha it will also be lined with men selling goats. It's a busy commercial approach to a holy place.

By Metro
To start the walk at the Meena Bazaar gate, take the Yellow Line to Chandni Chowk Metro Station and walk to Chandni Chowk; then get a scooter or cycle rickshaw to the start of your walk

on Subhash Chandra Bose Marg. You could, however, adapt the walk and get off at Chawri Bazaar Metro Station and walk up Chawri Bazaar itself to reach the rear of the Jama Masjid. With your back to Chawri Bazaar you then walk round the left-hand side of the mosque and pick up the walk at the Jama Masjid's main entrance gate for tourists (Gate 3).

The Walk

From Netaji Subhash Marg stop and look at the mosque as the view from the far end of the approach road is excellent. The dignity of the gateway, the delicacy of the minarets and the lovely symmetry of the domes make this building one of the most beautiful mosques in India. The modern approach road differs from the original seventeenth century one which was further over to your right at this point. However, look behind you at the Red Fort and mentally connect the gateway you can see with the mosque ahead.

Walk
2
ॐ〰ॐ

Imagine it's a Friday in 1657. Shah Jahan is going in procession in great magnificence from his palace fortress to his place of worship. There are hundreds of different kinds of soldiers, personal attendants, men carrying dark green pennants bearing golden suns, musicians on elephant-back beating kettledrums, and splendidly dressed nobles. The royal family are also on elephants, the royal ladies hidden from view in covered howdahs. The emperor himself sparkles with precious stones and pearls.

Begin to walk towards the mosque's massive gateway ahead of you, but after only 80 metres look out for a green metal gate on the right flanked by red sandstone gateposts. This was the entrance to one of Old Delhi's popular sporting venues called an akhara; an open-air wrestling ring. Now the Delhi Metro Corporation is using the space for storing its equipment and the wrestling has gone elsewhere. Look through the bars. You might have to squeeze behind a mothball seller who likes this patch in front of the gate. The site was a sandy square in the middle of a grassy amphitheatre where, on Sunday afternoons, wrestling matches would take place. On the gate there's a large green square which used to have a painting of two chubby young men pushing each other apart. (If you study it closely, under the green wash you can still see faint outlines of two chubby men pushing each other apart.) Many wrestlers are devotees of Hanuman, the Hindu God associated with strength and loyalty.

If it's a Friday or an Islamic feast day, the Jama Masjid main gate (Gate 2) will be open and the steps thronged with people. On other days, this imperial gateway is closed and only the north and south gateways are open to both Muslim worshippers and visitors. This walk assumes it's neither a Friday nor a feast day and guides you into the mosque through its northern gateway; Gate 3.

Stop at the end of the approach road before the first flight of steps. Turn left and walk along the central open section of the bazaar, then left again into the covered section of the Meena (Women's) Bazaar. The fabrics on sale here are expensive and therefore protected from the elements. This bazaar area is due for redevelopment as it is thought to be a fire hazard. In future years it may well be closed or significantly changed.

Walk
2
ॐॐॐ

The Meena Bazaar (The Women's Bazaar)

In 1976, during the Emergency, hundreds of dilapidated shack-type shops which huddled all around the mosque were demolished and lawns laid where once they'd stood. A few years later many of the dislodged shopkeepers were offered accommodation in the new Meena Bazaar. As this market sells mostly to Muslim ladies, or wholesale to Muslim shopkeepers, there are many shops selling the most wonderfully rich fabrics and fashionable burqas with sparkling designs on the front and at the cuffs. This is a new development! In the past burqas were always plain black but obviously younger fashionable Muslim girls want their share of bling. Bolts of cloth are piled high, with sequinned black velvets vying with delicate fabrics for the sparkle from the shop lights. Yet

Meena Bazaar in the 1980s

the shops aren't religiously mono-cultural as Hindu shopkeepers buy lengths from here too.

There are also household equipment shops and stalls for men selling little Muslim caps (topis), and pictures of sacred places. The places depicted are not all in Saudi Arabia. A popular subject is the shrine of Nizamuddin Auliya, the thirteenth century Islamic saint who's buried only a few miles south of here in the suburb of New Delhi that bears his name, Nizamuddin.

Retrace your way back through the Meena Bazaar to the foot of the first flight of steps and climb up on the right-hand side. There are thirty-two steps to the flat area at the top and both sides are cluttered with stalls, snack-sellers and soft-drinks trolleys.

The Sufi Shrines
Keep close to the right-hand side of the flight of steps as you climb to the top. There's a stall on the corner selling Islamic

religious cassettes (you can often hear the music before you reach his shop), a semi-precious stone dealer squatting on the ground with his rings and loose stones on a white cloth in front of him, and just behind him a souvenir clock shop. (Behind the hands of the clocks are pictures of Mecca or Koranic inscriptions.) After a few other stalls you'll see a low red and green painted building shaded by awnings and an overhanging tree. It contains two shrines. They are both shrines to Muslim martyrs and if you walk carefully between the people resting outside you can look through the pierced stone 'windows' and see the devout praying and kissing the flower-strewn graves. Beggars sit here too asking for alms.

Each martyr has his name written on the front of the building. The red shrine reveres the life of Hazrat Sufi Saeed Sarmad Saheed, a seventeenth century martyr who was born in Armenia to a Jewish family but converted to Islam. He was a great poet and Sufi mystic, and very popular with both ordinary people and with the nobles of the Mughal court. This popularity caused him to fear that he was losing contact with Allah so he decided to 'drop his clothes forever' and remained 'bare bodied' for the rest of his life. He became a martyr in the time of Aurangzeb as he was closely associated, as a spiritual advisor, with Darah Shikoh. Darah Shikoh was Aurangzeb's elder brother and rival for the throne. Aurangzeb had Darah Shikoh killed, and Sufi Sarmad not long after, on the grounds of holding unorthodox beliefs. The green shrine belongs to Hazrat Hare Bhare Shah who was the mentor of Hazrat Sufi Saeed Sarmad Saheed, his neighbour in the red shrine. Between the two on the front there's a board on which is written, in Urdu and English:

Walk
2
❦❧

'And call not those who
Are slain in the way of Allah "Dead".
Nay, they are living, only ye perceive not.'

The Walk to the Jama Masjid Entrance

Leave the shrines and continue to walk to the right of the Jama Masjid's Gate 2. Just a little way along the path you'll meet metal barriers. If you are in this area between 9 a.m. and 12.30 p.m. on a weekday, before walking through take a look at the activities happening on the flat space on your right behind a low wall topped by railings. This is the Dr Rahat's Open Surgery exercise area and you'll see people with tape tightly bound around certain limbs, exercising gently on benches. The limbs they are working on look rather like parcels. There is an explanatory metal post written by Dr Rahat (a hakeem, or traditional doctor) telling you how his system can improve your health and well-being. If it's a Sunday the area is taken over by goats.

Walk through the barrier and continue along the road which leads to the main tourist entrance to the Jama Masjid Gate 3. This stretch is known as 'Cotton Market Jama Masjid' and although you may see bales of cotton being used to stuff mattresses, there are far more shops selling new, modern mattresses and blankets in thick plastic covers lining either side of the road. The stalls on the right come to an end at two round, black, water tanks. From here to the end of the Cotton Market is a muddle of parked rickshaws, motorbikes and food stalls. At the end of the road you'll see a large, bright 'Shallesh Fireworks' sign across the road. Turn left here and walk along it for about 300 metres till it takes you to Gate 3 of the Jama Masjid. If you stay on the left you'll pass a police station, and just after it round the bend you'll see the large Gate 3 sign which is the gate you want.

Firework Shops

You have to cross over the road to see the firework shops. This is a 'No Smoking Zone' because of the danger of a spark causing an inferno. (There are 'No Smoking' signs up here and there but I don't know whether they are actually taken seriously.) It is evidently an old established firework bazaar as there's evidence of fireworks being sold here as long ago as the 1840s. All major Indian festivals need to go off with a bang so there's no shortage of customers selecting from the wonderfully named fireworks on offer. 'What would you like, sir? May I suggest ten Jasmine Flower Pot Rockets, twenty Golden Willows, fifteen Lunik Expresses and fifty Sparklers?' Diwali is bonanza time with each shop having crowds of customers jostling for service three deep.

On the opposite side of the road to the firework shops, huge, super clean air-conditioned tourist coaches inch in and out all day as they park to let their occupants get off to see the Jama Masjid. They fight for space with the humble rickshaws and porters pushing their laden barrows. The coaches seem to belong to a different world. Sadly, they effectively block the exit of the two fire engines you can see parked in the fire station behind them. One hopes fires in this extremely flammable area only occur at night! There are, of course, 'No Parking' signs on the fire station entrance gateways, but it's often hard to see them as they are hidden behind the coaches.

Walk
2
ॐ⊚ॐ

Gate 3 of the Jama Masjid

Entry is controlled by policemen and women. You walk through the arch of a metal detector and bags are searched. Climb the steps and take off your shoes and leave them with a man who will expect a certain sum for looking after them when you return. If you wish to take your camera with you there is a charge of 300 rupees which you pay to a man at the head of the steps. If you haven't got a camera but wish to climb the minaret you have to buy a separate ticket sold from the opposite gate, Gate 2—in which case you may pay a lower price. If you don't have a camera and don't want to climb the minaret, entrance is free. As soon as you point a camera at anything you may be asked to show your ticket. If your dress is regarded as immodest you will be asked to wear a brightly coloured wrap-around dress which is free. Sometimes unscrupulous men try to ask 100 rupees for them when you take them off but this is a scam. If your arms and legs are covered you need not wear one and this is preferable as the coveralls are hot. However you might have to fight the 'dealing-with-foreign-female-tourists-en-masse' mindset to succeed!

The Jama Masjid (The Friday Mosque, 1656)

The Jama Masjid was originally called 'The mosque commanding a view of the world' (Masjid-i-Jahanuma) as it was built on a rocky outcrop higher than the surrounding land.

As you walk around you'll appreciate the advantage of this extra height, as there are excellent views across the city from the courtyard arcades. The building does command Old Delhi, but as for 'the world', one has to dismiss this claim as just another example of the boundlessness of Mughal hyperbole! In many ways, the Jama Masjid was a Mughal Westminster Abbey, as all the emperors—from Auranzeb in the seventeenth century to the last Mughal emperor, Bahadur Shah Zafar, in the mid-nineteenth— were crowned here by the highest Muslim dignitary in the land, the Shahi Imam. In constructing the mosque, special care was taken to ensure that the level of the pulpit in the mosque was higher than that of the royal throne used by the emperor in the Red Fort. It's the largest mosque in India.

The Jama Masjid was begun in 1650 by Shah Jahan and took 5,000 men six years to complete. If mosques were gems, this would be the Koh-i-Noor.

Turn left immediately after entering Gate 3, and walk under, if you can, or parallel to if you can't, the left-hand side arcade. You're walking towards a large, white, ornately carved wooden structure which looks a little like a big white wardrobe. (Sadly, occasionally this arcade is completely fenced off and then the relics can't be seen.)

The Relics of the Prophet Mohammed

If the white structure is locked but the arcade open, and you'd like to see its contents, the keeper's room is nearby in the middle of the arcade. You are most likely to be approached and asked if you'd like to see the relics, but if there's no one around walk to the keeper's room and make yourself known. The keepers change, but all of them are pleased to show the relics to visitors. The relics are regarded as being the most precious contents of the mosque and treated with great reverence.

You will be told about the relics as you are shown them. There are two very old Korans written on deerskin, in Kufic script, by a son-in-law and a grandson of the Prophet, one long red hair from the Prophet's beard, now kept in a glass vial, and his sandals, hardly visible, so embedded in jasmine flowers. However, the mosque's greatest treasure is produced last, and that's a footprint of the Prophet in marble. If you have joined a group of Indian Muslim visitors to the mosque then you will see the faithful kissing the footprint and mothers stroking the smooth marble footprint then running their hands over their babies' heads to pass on the blessing. It's a touching sight. After viewing the relics a donation to the mosque is always acceptable although not usually requested directly. Rupee notes are often squeezed into the sides of the relic containers.

Walk
2

Leave this arcade and turn 90 degrees to walk along the arcade which faces the Red Fort. After looking outwards, turn round and a few metres into the courtyard is a squat, one metre high, rectangular red stone with a map of the world on the top. It dates from the mid-nineteenth century.

The Jama Masjid Courtyard

Walk further into the courtyard and stand facing the three-storey gatehouse which is over the mosque's Imperial Gateway—today's Gate 2—the entrance to which is usually locked. There's a delicate covered balcony projecting high over the central gateway and in Mughal times this is where the royal ladies sat, hidden from view, but able to follow the service. They could see clearly into the prayer hall from their high vantage point. The alcoves in the gatehouse would have been occupied by guards.

Walk towards the central pool. You'll see a pipe on the far side from which water pours constantly, for this is an ablution tank and has to contain running water. (In the past, there were fountains in the tank.) Before praying, a Muslim will wash his hands and feet and rinse his mouth. There is a channel around the edge of the pool for receiving the water used for rinsing your mouth.

The pillars at the four corners of the pool are lamp posts.

You can see two raised platforms from here. They're called 'dikkas'. A dikka is platform on which a man sits copying the movements of the prayer leader (the Imam) and chanting the service in unison with him. He keeps the ordinary worshipper in the courtyard in touch with the Imam in the prayer hall. These dikkas are not very old as a painting of the Jama Masjid in the 1840s doesn't show either of them. It's unusual to see two dikkas in a mosque, but this courtyard is so vast, and so many people pray here, that two are needed. Every Friday about 30,000 attend and for special feast days there are 85,000 of the faithful in and around the mosque. As you climbed up to the mosque you may have noticed short white lines on the steps. These aren't decorative but needed

Red Fort from Jama Masjid, c. 1870. Photographer: Saché

Walk
2

to ensure that each worshipper has enough space to pray when the courtyard is full, and the overspill lay their prayer mats on the steps. The men in the courtyard, following the Imam's movements, are helped by the height and whiteness of the Imam's distinctive turban, which makes his head movements always easily identifiable.

The ablution tank next to you was once threatened with obliteration. When the British closed the mosque after the 1857 Uprising, they turned it into a barracks for the Punjab Infantry. The British military people found the pool got in the way and wanted to fill it in, but the head of the civil authorities wouldn't let them and later moved the soldiery out to cattle sheds in Daryaganj.

Enter the prayer hall itself, on the far side of the pool under the domes. Look at the superb craftsmanship of inlaid marble on red sandstone on the walls and especially under the cusped arches.

On either side of and above the central niche—the mihrab— are two round patterns called roundels. Each says 'Ya Gaffer', a prayerful call to God, many times. The repetitions make the pattern. The low marble pulpit on the right of the niche has a finely carved left-hand side made out of a single block of marble. The Imam never stands on the top step but always delivers his sermons from the one beneath. The top one is kept vacant in respectful memory of the Prophet Mohammed giving his sermons from the top one. The large ornate chandelier is a recent addition.

As you walk through the carpeted prayer hall, you'll see piles of Korans in Urdu on bookshelves. Nowadays anyone can borrow a Koran and worship within the prayer hall. In Shah Jahan's time only the nobles were allowed to pray here, and they did so by kneeling on silk carpets covering the marble floor.

Walk into the courtyard and look up at the outside of the large central arch. You'll see two more roundels, also calling to God, but with a different invocation. This time it's 'Ya Hadi'.

The writing in Arabic, in the ten oblongs above the arches facing the courtyard, isn't religious but historical. These inscriptions give information about the building of the mosque itself.

It probably isn't written above an arch but it's certainly a well-known fact that Shah Jahan shocked the supervisors of his works in 1656, by telling them that he intended to use the mosque the following day to celebrate a major Islamic festival. Their hearts must have sunk as they thought it far from ready. However they did not panic. They let it be known throughout the city that anyone could come and take away anything he wanted that he saw lying around. The courtyard was emptied of tons of rubble and surplus building material in a few hours. The following day, the new mosque was magnificently decorated and lit, ready for Shah Jahan's inaugural visit.

Climbing the Minaret

Cross the courtyard to the southern gateway—Gate 1—directly opposite Gate 3, the one you came in by. It's from this southern gate that you begin the climb to the top of the minaret. If you have a 300 rupee ticket, a mosque employee will check it and show you the entrance. (There is a man selling minaret tickets on this side of the courtyard but these are only for people who haven't bought the 300 rupee ticket.)

There are said to be 123 steps, and the climb and return take about twenty minutes. Before reaching the minaret you walk along the top of the mosque wall following a path marked by canvas matting. If wearing a Jama Masjid wrap-around dress, you might find it easier to climb if you tie it around your waist. At the base of the minaret itself the 'minaret guide' will check your ticket and offer his services. Once you reach the top of the minaret, you enter a small open pavilion surrounded by a low marble balcony on top of which has been constructed a modern metal safety grill. It is cooler up there in the summer and the ledge can get quite crowded as visitors sit around chatting, looking over the old city and enjoying the breeze. It's a wonderful place to take photographs. Descend the minaret, cross back to Gate 3 where you left your shoes, collect them and give the shoe-man his tip.

He will remind you if you don't.

Stop for a minute at the top of the steps and look over the area of the city you see ahead of you. The bulk of Old Delhi's Hindu population lives in this northern part of the city. The Hindu cremation ground and the river Yamuna ghats (bathing steps) are all north of here. The opposite would be true if you were standing on the steps of Gate 1 looking south. From here the view would be of an overwhelmingly Muslim part of Old Delhi. From birth to death you need never leave your own community.

Walk down the steps, leave the mosque and turn left following the road round the back of the mosque. There's a lot of bamboo scaffolding for hire just in front of the railings of the mosque's rear wall. The extremely busy road facing the rear of the mosque is Chawri Bazaar.

Chawri Bazaar

The name 'Chawri' is a Marathi word for the meeting place in front of a great noble's house, where the noble would sit on a low platform and try to settle disputes, before they could be taken to a higher authority, the emperor, in the Red Fort. One glance down Chawri Bazaar will convince you that this street is no longer occupied by twentieth century equivalents of great nobles! However, in the eighteenth century there were several huge mansions here. The present character of the street's architecture is predominantly late nineteenth century. After the Uprising (1857), the British destroyed some of the old buildings in Chawri Bazaar and straightened the road. In the nineteenth century, Chawri Bazaar became famous for its 'dancing girls', many of whom had other talents as well. But not all. Some of the women were highly esteemed artists and wouldn't consider prostitution. The girls aren't there now. Delhi Municipal Committee moved in and moved them out. There's a pretty balcony on the right-hand side above Man Singh & Co., next to Shop No. 1012 Chawri Bazaar, where it is still just about possible to imagine slim, beautiful

Chawri Bazaar in the 1980s

'dancing' girls giggling to each other and flirting with the men below.

If you look up, you will see a mass of cables. It's an amazing tangle but it is planned that eventually all the cables will be placed underground. Improvements have taken place already as the cables used to be live and it was easy for people to make 'irregular' connections and steal electricity. This can't happen nowadays as the cables have been insulated. For techies, the orange cables carry fibre optic connections for telephone and internet usage.

With your back to the Jama Masjid, walk down the right-hand side of Chawri Bazaar. It's a very crowded street. Amongst the first small shops are wholesale and retail copper and brass goods and you'll soon come to Man Singh & Co. with its pretty nineteenth century balcony above. The metal shops stock Buddhas, Vishnus and Krishnas, brass ladies, bells, shields, oil lamps, vases, planters for plant-pots, ornate boxes, masks and ashtrays. Although most of their custom is wholesale, the shopkeepers are happy to sell you one brass planter or a Buddha if you ask.

Walk
2
৪⊙⊘৪

Intermingling with the brass shops, and soon taking over completely, are the wholesale paper and wedding stationery shops. Ganesh, the elephant-headed God appears on most of the cards in one form or another (even if it's just the swirl of a trunk) as he is the God of weddings. The swastik sign is popular too as it symbolizes a happy married life. Most of the cards are aimed at the Hindu wedding market, although, like the Meena Bazaar shops, they are not mono-cultural and have cards for Muslim, Sikh and Jain weddings too. Order in hundreds. You only have sixty people coming to your wedding? Not good enough! The minimum purchase is 100 cards and of course an average Hindu wedding would involve 200 or 300 guests or even more. Some Bollywood stars invite thousands! Keep walking along and cross over a small lane entering from the right. Walk past many more shops selling either metals or paper until you see an old dead tree rising above a lot of stalls built against its base. It's just after Shop

No. 2426-28: Gulshan Rai Bir Sain Jain (All Kind Envelope). The wide street that enters here from the right is Nai Sarak and is the one you want. Walk along a little and check that you are in the right street by reading the addresses on the shops' signs. Nai Sarak is a very well-known street, so if you have turned right too early, ask a shopkeeper to point you in the right direction.

Nai Sarak (New Street)

This long straight street was new over a hundred years ago. The British cut through a maze of older buildings to construct the road after the Uprising of 1857.

As with Chawri Bazaar, most of its character is nineteenth and twentieth century; an incredible squash of stationery and bookshops, some only as big as cupboards, but every inch filled with books or rulers, erasers, and notebooks, is to be found here. If you enjoy reading, you might imagine a street of bookshops to be your idea of heaven. But Nai Sarak is disappointing in this sense as the bookshops aren't for browsers. The shopkeepers are wholesalers as well as retailers and they haven't the space for browsers. To obtain a book you tell an assistant the title and he passes it to you. Most of the customers know what they are looking for and make for special shops. The trade is divided up; some shops specialize in Hindi literature, others children's books or medical textbooks, and there are many stocking second-hand paperbacks. The vast majority of the shops are very well-organized, but one or two are so crowded you wonder how the shopkeepers ever find anything. But they must. They stay in business.

About halfway up Nai Sarak, you'll notice that the book and stationery shops give way to wholesale and retail sari shops and red and gold bridal veil specialists. The range of types, colours and designs of the saris is stunning and those knowledgeable about saris or textiles spend hours here. If you like textiles then this area is for you. Notice that the newer bride mannequins usually have their eyes modestly looking downwards, as would a traditional

Indian bride on her wedding day, whereas the older, paler-skinned mannequin-brides stare dumbly ahead.

If you are not too interested in this section, walk as briskly as you can to Chandni Chowk. Your walk ends opposite the Town Hall.

Take a cycle or scooter rickshaw back to your car at the Red Fort's Delhi Gate or cross the road and make for the Chandni Chowk Metro Station.

Walk
2
ೞ⊚ೞ⊚ೞ

Walk 3:
Wings and Weddings

Birds, bridegrooms, and beautiful Jain temples. A weekday morning or early evening walk through narrow lanes and jostling crowds.

Places of Interest

DIGAMBARA JAIN TEMPLE (LAL MANDIR) (Open 6 a.m.-12 p.m. and again from 6 p.m. to 9.30 p.m.)
JAIN BIRD HOSPITAL (Open 8 a.m. to 9 p.m.)
SILVER STREET (DARIBA KALAN)
WEDDING STREET (KINARI BAZAAR)
JAIN SVETAMBARA TEMPLE
GHANTEWALA (an old sweet shop)

Getting There

By Car
Park in the large, well-organized and well-known Red Fort car park in front of the fort's Delhi Gate. It's approached from Nishad Raj Marg. Charges vary according to length of stay but are always reasonable. Then take a cycle or auto rickshaw to Chandni Chowk. Stop in front of a big red Jain temple called Lal Mandir.

By Metro
Take the Yellow Line to Chandni Chowk Metro Station and walk to the street itself. Exit from Gate 5. It is signposted 'Chandni

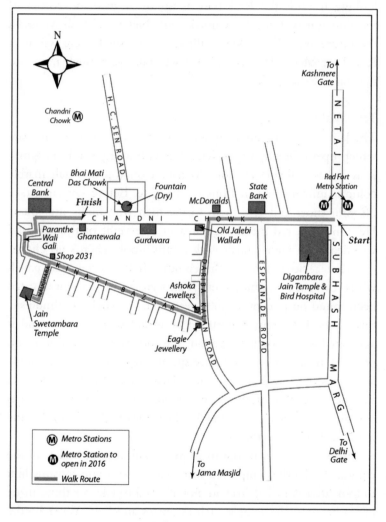

Walk 3: Route Map

Chowk'. Once on the street, and with your back to the shops, look left and you'll see the Red Fort at the end of the road. Take a cycle or auto rickshaw to the Jain temple—Lal Mandir—which, looking towards the Red Fort, is on the right-hand corner of the junction of Chandni Chowk with Netaji Subhash Marg. In the future, once Delhi Metro Phase 3 is finished, there will be a Red Fort Metro Station and this will take you much nearer to the start of this walk.

The Walk

The Jain temple has three entrances. Please enter by the main gate which opens directly onto Netaji Subhash Marg. You'll recognize it as it has a shrine to Lord Mahavira on top of a tall marble column immediately in front of the gate. Before entering, take off your shoes and give them to the man who looks after them. He controls a red metal cage area on the right of the gate and will deal with your sandals with a nifty hook. There's no charge.

Take a closer look at the column. It has rectangular panels which carry the swastik pattern. This sign is truly ancient as it has been found on pots over 2,000 years old. Generally, in Hinduism, this mystical diagram is regarded as an aid to meditation and is associated with good health, a long life and prosperity. A translation of 'swast' means 'it is well'. More specifically, here in a Jain temple it is associated with the seventh Tirthankara Suparsvanatha. In Europe a version of this sign, adopted by the Nazi party, has completely eradicated its much older meaning. Pass under the metal security detector arch.

With your back to the main road, walk round the left of the column to another employee who will beckon you towards him to look after your bag. You are not allowed to take anything made of leather into the temple such as purses and belts. Water bottles are banned too. There's no photography allowed so your camera has to be left behind as well.

Digambara Jain Temple

Before climbing the steps into the temple, find somewhere to sit and read a little about the temple and Jainism. This Jain temple itself has a very long history. The original temple was built in 1656 but there have been additions and modifications made ever since. In the 1800s there was a lot of new building done and the temple was further enlarged in the 1870s. The founder of Jainism is called Mahavira and he lived in the sixth century BC in an area of India now called Bihar. Mahavira (the great hero) also has another name, 'Jina' (the conqueror), and the name of the religion is derived from this. Mahavira was a prince who renounced everything to search for the meaning of life. Jains don't believe Mahavira to be the only founder of their religion, however. They say that he was the last of twenty-four 'ford-finders' (Tirthankaras) who help one to bridge the divide between the earthly and the divine. It is these Tirthankaras you see being worshipped in Jain temples. There are two branches of Jainism, and followers of the Digambara branch uphold the belief that being 'sky clad' or naked, (Digambara means sky-clad), i.e., just wearing, as they say 'the environment' like Lord Mahavira, is the best. Nowadays, only Jain ascetics practise total nakedness. Everyone you meet inside will be clothed. Climb the steps up to the terrace on the first floor.

Walk
3
৯৩৴৩৯

Inside the Temple

As long as your behaviour is sober, respectful and unobtrusive you are very welcome to enter all the rooms of the temple. The terrace leads into a spacious devotional area which is always busy. People sit at little tables on which may be offerings of rice, almonds, cloves and fragments of coconut, quietly praying or reading holy texts. You may see that the rice has been made into swastik patterns. Here it is a devotional device to help people meditate. There are an overwhelming number of silver and gilt shrines, and magnificent painted ceilings, and leading off from the main room are eight smaller rooms devoted to different Tirthankaras. This temple is dedicated to Lord Parshwnath, the twenty-third Titrthankara, who lived 250 years before Lord Mahavira. It is difficult for the non-Jain to distinguish between the different Tirthankaras. However, the shrines to Lord Parshwnath are easily recognizable as he has a cobra's hood acting as a canopy above his head. All the shrines are busy centres of religious activity with devotees making offerings, lighting individual ghee lamps or praying. As in Hindu temples, the busiest times at the temple are in the early morning for prayers or puja, or evenings at 7 p.m. for aarti, the religious ritual during which the deities are circled with lights from wicks soaked in ghee. In the evening the priests lead the chanting of bhajans—devotional songs. You'll notice that in a Jain temple the men and women pray together side by side in a respectful but relaxed way.

Walk
3
ॐ

Jains are noted for their aversion to killing anything that lives, however humble, and for having very strict dietary laws. Jains not only refuse to eat any form of meat but also any vegetable that has been grown underground such as potatoes, horseradish and carrots. Even onions and garlic are forbidden. Their aversion to killing means that some Jains wear masks to prevent them from accidentally swallowing flying insects; as you walk about Old Delhi you'll see some Jain shopkeepers wearing them. Evidence for this concern for life can be found just above you. Look up and you'll notice that each ceiling fan is carefully caged and pigeons perch confidently on the temple chandeliers.

Leave the main temple area and descend the steps. Collect your bag and walk over to the well-signposted Bird Hospital. As you cross the forecourt, you may see monkeys gravely patrolling the perimeter walls.

Jain Bird Hospital

It's very easy to identify, as there is a delightful painting of both injured and healthy birds flying around a magnifying glass enlargement of the hospital's interior. The hospital is an amazing place. It's very clean and extremely busy with a total in-patient count of about 3,000 birds. Because the hospital floors are often sluiced, expect to be paddling about the corridors at times. If you can't handle wet feet don't investigate further! The very sick birds have their own cages, whereas the convalescents share. Fully recovered birds are given their freedom on Saturdays. The medical staff can tell when birds are fully recovered because they fly about a lot and perch on the upper racks in the convalescent rooms. Most of the patients are pigeons, although you sometimes see peacocks, parrots and birds of prey. The latter are always given their own cages.

The staff are dedicated and most welcoming. There isn't an entrance fee but they do appreciate a donation. There's a Visitor's Book for you to sign and some amusing comments from others to read. One from a Dutch visitor: 'Preep-preep. I try to say something for the birds' and a wry one from a British tourist: 'I hope they all pull through'.

If you are interested in Jain religious tales ask someone to explain the complicated story behind the series of gruesome paintings at reception. Briefly, they show a man who has cut off part of his own arm and leg and put them on one half of a scale to balance the weight of a bird, in order to prevent the bird being eaten by a hawk. (In fact, the birds were both Gods in disguise and the man was simply being tested, so all ends happily—according to Jain mythology.) Leave the Jain temple complex. There's a Jain book and gift shop on the ground floor over on the right, near to a large, silver-painted wrought-iron gate.

The Walk to Dariba Kalan

With your back to the temple's main gate, turn left. As you walk past the temple railings you'll see posters of present-day Jain ascetics, all men, all naked, maintaining their modesty with a crossed leg, bent arm or strategically placed peacock feather broom! The only two personal possessions Jain ascetics are allowed is a water gourd and a feather broom. Keep walking left and you're soon in Chandni Chowk. Walk past the Gauri Shankar Hindu temple and the stalls selling all that is needed to worship there: marigolds, rose petals, bilva leaves and cotton thread candles in tiny clay bowls. After the temple there are about twenty-five small shops selling shoes, bags and clothing. There's a photographic store Marlan Jee and Co. at the end of this row, so pause here for a minute and look at the wide road that's in front of you. It's Esplanade Road—a road with a British name and of British creation. It's so straight that it's very unlike most of the winding roads west of it and this is because it was built much later. After the Uprising of 1857, the British demolished a lot of seventeenth century mansions near the fort to give the guns (now British controlled) a clear firing line into the town from their positions on the walls of the Red Fort. The word 'esplanade' derives from the Latin 'explanare', meaning 'to flatten', and the British certainly did this to the properties near the fort! Esplanade Road was the demarcation line between the military area centred in the Red Fort and the civil area of the town.

Cross over Esplanade Road and walk for a further 150 metres; you'll walk the latter part of the way under a veranda. Turn left at the lane immediately in front of the Old Famous Jalebi Wala, a well-know jalebi snack shop. Jalebis are curly fried syrupy sweets. Delicious! You are now in Dariba Kalan.

Dariba Kalan (The Street of the Incomparable Pearl)

Although popularly known as Silver Street by foreign visitors, the word 'Dariba' is the result of running together the words in the Persian phrase 'Dur-e be-baha' which means 'pearl without compare.' Kalan simply means large. Silver doesn't feature at all except in the many jewellers' shop windows but undoubtedly today's trade is more silver dominated than pearl.

Where Dariba Kalan meets Chandni Chowk there used to

be a gate across the road. There's no sign of it now but it was called the Khooni Darwaza or the Bloody Gate. In 1739, the Persian king Nadir Shah defeated the Mughal emperor of the time (Mohammed Shah) at the battle of Karnal. Nadir Shah then marched to Delhi.

In 1739, this trading street was full of jewellery, pearls, gold and silver, just as it is now, so that when Nadir Shah ordered a general slaughter of Delhi's citizenry his soldiers were particularly keen to slaughter here and loot as well. Hundreds of bodies were said to have littered the street and they piled up against the gates. There are further details of this terrible day in Delhi's life at the end of the walk.

The jewellery shops have the loveliest necklaces, earrings and bracelets, traditional and modern. There's a tradition amongst the shopkeepers in this old street that they do better trade if they keep their safe doors open. As you walk along you'll notice this to be true. You'll see many instances of a shop-owner sitting at the back of his shop in front of a large open safe. I doubt it would happen in London's Hatton Garden!

To find Kinari Bazaar walk down Dariba Kalan and take the fourth opening on your right.

Walk
3

Dariba Kalan in the 1980s

It's about 200 metres from Chandni Chowk. It's very easy to find as it's the only side lane with a metal arch above it saying Kinari Bazaar in Hindi. You'll know you've entered Kinari Bazaar as it has a mass of small, very brightly bedecked shops full of garlands and fancy goods needed for weddings. As a further check, Eagle Jewellery is the corner shop on the left and Ashoka Jewellers on the right.

Wedding Street—Kinari Bazaar

Foreigners know this street as 'Wedding Street' when the meaning of 'kinari' is really 'ornate edging or braid'. Not that it matters as the important thing is to walk down this old street and enjoy the glitz and glitter of gold and red, garlands and wedding paraphernalia. Here you see prospective bridegrooms self-consciously trying on gold lame wedding turbans, brides choosing hair decorations and relatives buying currency note garlands to give to the groom on his big day. Although much is traditional in Kinari Bazaar there are some new developments; the fancy, gauzy gift packaging shops have grown in number and modernization is taking place as some of the shops have installed air conditioning. This puts an end to the traditional open-fronted style of shop where the shop owner controls everything as he sits cross-legged at the front of the shop on a white, cloth-covered bolster. Fortunately, the photogenic nature of the street has yet to be seriously dented.

Walk
3
ॐ✿ॐ

In the months of July and August, weddings take a back seat to the little cotton bracelets known as rakhis that sisters give to their brothers, symbolizing her prayers for her brother's well-being and his lifelong vow to protect her. They are usually red, or mostly red, to avert evil and the sisters get a present from their brothers in exchange. In October, the whole street is magical as the shops are not only stocked with wedding season goods but also the bows and arrows for 'Ram Lila', a folk play about the Hindu hero Rama. This is the time to see the mounds of extra heads for the evil king Ravana and enough cardboard swords for hundreds of school armies.

The Walk to Naughara

Walk along Kinari Bazaar for about 400 metres because you are now walking towards a cul-de-sac called Naughara (nine houses). It's the eighth opening on your left, but don't worry too much if you lose count. It's a well-known place and shopkeepers will always waft you further along or send you back if you miss it. As a further check you need to turn left opposite Shop No. 2031 Kinari Bazaar: Krishna & Co. Gote Wala. Naughara is very distinctive. It's a pleasure to see the bright colours of the painted doorways on your right and the freshness of the pot plants in front of them. They go some way to compensate for the smell coming from the urinal just behind the gate on the left! The Jain Svetambara temple is at the end on the right but not easily visible from the gate.

Naughara (Nine Houses)

There used to be many little nineteenth century streets like this in Old Delhi, with a gate they could close in the evenings, and their own well, but sadly many have disappeared. Most of the nine houses are occupied by Jain families and one extended family (Nahar) occupy four of the nine. They are families of jewellers. Walk to the temple at the end on the right.

The Jain Svetambara Temple and the Svetambara Branch of Jainism

The temple is open to non-worshippers and tourists, from 9 a.m. to 8 p.m. The Jains are split into two main groups. The large temple you first visited was a Digambara (sky-clad) temple. This one belongs to the other group, the Svetambaras (white-clad). However, both believe in the Jain principles of universal brotherhood, forgiveness, and love and compassion for all living things. Traditionally, the differences relate to the wearing of clothes. The Digambaras believe that to obtain nirvana (salvation) you shouldn't wear clothes at all. The Svetambaras believe this is impractical in today's world and that you can obtain nirvana but the clothes should be white.

Enter the temple leaving your shoes and any other leather items you may possess on the ground floor. It's a Jain practice to wash your hands after handling shoes, and also rinse your mouth before entering the temple. There is a washbasin nearby and it is appreciated if you do carry out these cleansing practices, although not dogmatically insisted upon. You will be handed a list of rules at the entrance, one of which, Rule 2, you might find discriminatory. Who's to know? Climb the staircase. As in the Jain temple you visited earlier, the main devotional hall is on the first floor.

Inside the Temple

One of the most startling images you see as you walk around the first floor is a large black carving of a Tirthankara (Jain saint) you may have seen before in the Digambara temple. He's the twenty-third of the line, Lord Parshwnath. The main shrine has five Tirthankara images. In the centre is Lord Suminath; to his right and left are images of the same man Lord Adinath; and to the left and right of Lord Adinath, are Lord Ajitnath and Lord Neminath respectively. It's all rather confusing. What is easier to follow is the morning ritual during which a priest bathes the images of the Tirthankaras in milk, then water, and finally their feet are anointed with a paste made of sandalwood and saffron.

There are shrines to other Tirthankaras around the temple. As you walk around the first floor, notice two shrine niches that have strong, locked silver gates. One is on your right at the head of the staircase and contains a shapeless stone that has a silver face and wears a gold crown, with a gold canopy over it. This stone represents Bhaironji to whom Jains pray to help them keep

A Jain Tirthankara

trouble away. Bhaironji isn't a Tirthankara himself but their loyal and obedient servant. He is said to have a role similar to that of Hanuman in Hinduism.

On the opposite wall, the left-hand side, the locked silver gates protect small images of Tirthankaras studded with precious stones and diamonds. This Jain temple is often known as 'the jewellers' temple' so it's not surprising that jewel-encrusted Tirthankaras are found here. The whole temple is beautifully cared for and obviously cherished. But the best has yet to come, a storey higher and at the far end. Climb the second flight of stairs. In the first room you come to, you can trace the life—in nineteenth or early twentieth century coloured glass mosaic—of Lord Mahavira. If your back is to the street, you may trace the story of his life such, that it starts with his birth (middle of the left-hand side wall) and ends with him blessing people from heaven, on the back wall.

The highlight is still to come. Walk to the far end of the top floor and look up at the ceiling where there are some superb early Mughal style paintings of dancers and musicians. It almost looks as though they were painted on the roof to entertain the small, solemn, naked Tirthankaras below! The finely painted gold work on their three-tiered marble pedestal is exquisite. Clear glass now protects the panels from modern wear and tear, yet doesn't stop its beauty from shining through. Here, in the oldest part of the temple, you can perhaps imagine more easily than anywhere else in Old Delhi what the interiors of the palaces in the Red Fort must have looked like when new.

This Jain temple now operates a small Jain kitchen called a Bhojan Shala. If you'd like to sample Jain snacks please talk to the secretary, Mr Vinay Chand Sankhwal Jain, and he'll get some prepared. Mr Jain can be found sitting just behind the entrance to the temple on a raised platform. He's there every day welcoming visitors and keeping an eye on things. Donations are always gratefully received.

As you walk back through Naughara, to the crush and din
of Kinari Bazaar, enjoy the quietness here. It doesn't last. At the
mouth of this cul-de-sac turn left, and continue walking along.
The shops at this end of the street better reflect the translation
of the street's name; yards and yards of braid. Keep left until the
narrow street of Kinari Bazaar opens up and there's a road to your
right. It's easy to spot if you look down, as it has unusual red and
yellow wavy paving stones covering the road surface. Turn into
the road. This is Paranthe Wali Gali. You'll see a sign on the right,
'Birbal Das and Co', and another for 'Babu Ram'. This is the road
you want as it'll lead you back to Chandni Chowk.

Paranthe Wali Gali and Paranthas

This road is part of Paranthe Wali Gali—the street of the parantha
sellers. A parantha is a special kind of flat unleavened bread. It
can be round or triangular, sometimes stuffed and always fried
in either ghee (clarified butter) or oil. You can see them being
made at Pt (Pandit) Gaya Prasad Shiv Charan's Cafe. His sign
says it all—'an experience of 5 generations'—although when you
talk to the present owner he says it's now six! His busy little
restaurant must be quite similar to when his great, great, great
grandfather set up in business. The place has a distinctly old-
fashioned air about it even today. Paranthas are very filling, and
therefore popular snacks as well as often being eaten at breakfast
time. Try one if you're hungry.

Walk
3

This lane brings you out opposite a regional office of the
Central Bank. Look to the right and you'll see the Red Fort.
Turn right and stay on the right-hand side of Chandni Chowk if
you're fond of traditional Indian sweets. There's a famous old shop
called Ghantewala, established in 1790, selling the most delicious
varieties. It is Shop No. 1862 and about 80 metres from your exit.
It shares its shop number with the glitzy sari shop Roop Saree
Creation as Ghantewala once used to be bigger—before they cut
themselves in two. They kept the bell.

Ghantewala Sweet Shop

Ghantewala means 'Bell Ringer' and there are several explanations for the name. The most likely is that the shop owner or his assistants jingled bells to attract customers from the throng passing by. However, there's another more interesting story. In Mughal times there were great processions along Chandni Chowk and it's said that the royal elephant would stop in front of this shop and ring its bell, refusing to go further until it was given some sweets. Whatever the reason, there is, above the main sweet counter facing the road, an old, ornate brass bell.

It's certainly true that Ghantewala sweets were supplied to Mughal royalty; and the recipes haven't changed at all since those Mughal times.

If you've never tasted this kind of sweet before try a quarter of a kilo of one or two varieties, such as sohan halwa, a large toffee ring made of cornflour, sugar and ghee, with nuts on the top; kaju-ki-barfi, a cashewnut fudge; laddus, small balls made of flour, ghee, and brown sugar, rolled in nuts; and pinni, sweets made from boiled-down milk called khoya.

There are many more—emarti, kajwar, cashew-roll, tirangi-barfi, kaju-standard, sohan-pabri, parmal, and pista-loj. Gently resting on top of the sweets and sparkling in the sunshine is the edible silver-leaf called vark.

Your walk ends here.

Take a cycle or auto rickshaw back to your car or cross the road and make for the Chandni Chowk Metro Station. Taxis are available in front of Old Delhi Railway Station (Delhi Main).

If you'd like a drink or a snack before doing so, there's a shop a few hundred metres further down on the other side of the street called Haldiram's. It's easy to spot as there's a large HALDIRAM'S sign above the sweet shop it operates below. Upstairs, there's a vegetarian cafe selling a range of Indian snacks such as raj kachori and international meals such as cheese burgers and pizza. It's a busy place. Fortunately, there are many waiters

Walk
3
ॐ

so you are served quickly. If it is the summer time, and you've never tried a traditional Indian cooling drink, there are two for sale here: mango panna and kesar thandai. The first involves green mangoes, mint and spices, and the second, cooling seeds, ground almonds and saffron, and both are delicious. They are served in disposable plastic cups.

Historical Appendix

Nadir Shah's Slaughter of Delhi's Population in 1739

On 7 March 1739, the Persian king Nadir Shah arrived outside Delhi and made his army camp outside the city walls. The next day Nadir Shah entered the Red Fort with 200 servants and 4,000 horsemen and was graciously received and entertained by the defeated emperor, Mohammed Shah.

For four days there wasn't any trouble. Nadir Shah controlled his troops with the most horrible punishments. They would lose their noses and ears or be beaten to death if they molested or robbed any local citizens.

Trouble began when the Persians ordered Delhi's city granaries to be opened to feed their men and then refused to pay the merchants the normal price for wheat. A mob gathered and killed some of the Persians who'd come to take the wheat. (This was the evening of Saturday, 10 March 1739). Overnight the mob got angrier and bigger and started arming itself. There was also a rumour that Nadir Shah had been taken prisoner, or poisoned, and this put greater vigour into the Delhi mob's efforts. More Persians died. About 8 o'clock on Sunday morning the city was in such turmoil that Nadir Shah left the Red Fort on horseback and tried, through his presence, to calm things down. On the way he saw some of his countrymen lying dead and, what's more, a local citizen with a musket shot at him, missed, but killed one of his officers near him. Nadir Shah's anger knew no bounds. He ordered his troops to slaughter the local people. By 3 o'clock on that Sunday afternoon, more than 30,000 of Delhi's citizenry were dead. Two months later, in May 1739, Nadir Shah left the Delhi he'd ruined. He returned to Persia with his army and a huge baggage train carrying the treasures of the city he'd so thoroughly sacked. These included the Koh-i-Noor diamond and the magnificent Peacock Throne.

Walk
3
ಕ೮ಳ೮ಕ

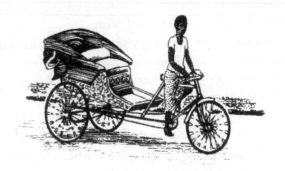

Walk **4**:
Walled City Gateways

Mughal gateways to a Queen of Delhi's tomb and lively, colourful streets with house facades from earlier times. This is an any-time-of-day walk. This is one of the longer walks so allow two hours.

The Madrasa and Tomb of Ghazi-uddin are very well worth seeing and in the past have been easily accessible. However, at present you need to write a brief letter stating your name and saying that you'd like permission to see the Madrasa and Tomb of Ghazi-uddin. Write to; The Secretary, Delhi Education Society, The Anglo Arabic Senior Secondary School, Ajmeri Gate, New Delhi 110006. (New Delhi includes Old Delhi for postal purposes.) You will receive a letter in reply giving you permission. This system may change in the future, and foreign visitors may be allowed in more easily, but at present this isn't the case.

Places of Interest
TURKMAN GATE
HOLY TRINITY CHURCH
DARGAH OF SHAH TURKMAN BAYABANI
KALAN MASJID
SULTAN RAZIA'S TOMB
AJMERI GATE
THE MADRASA AND TOMB OF GHAZI-UDDIN (If you have gained permission)

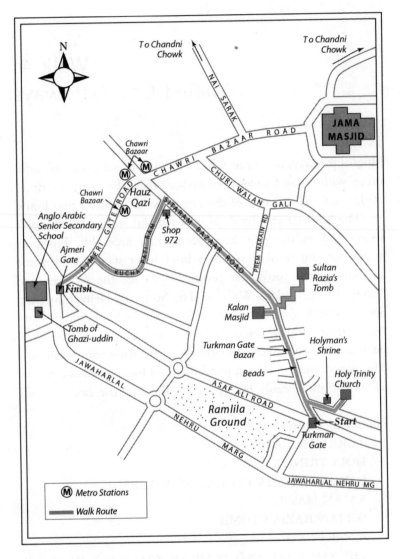

Walk 4: Route Map

Getting There

By Car

You can park on one side of Asif Ali Road if you arrive not later than 9.30 a.m. Many of the spaces on this rough unofficial site are reserved for businessmen who pay a retainer to the man who organizes the parking. This is why he sometimes won't let you park even though there are spaces available.

Otherwise, park in the Red Fort Delhi Gate car park and get a cycle or auto rickshaw to the start of your walk at Turkman Gate.

By Metro

New Delhi Metro Station is your nearest Metro station.

The Walk

Stand facing Turkman Gate. It was built in 1658 and looks small nowadays as it has lost its adjoining walls, and its red sandstone and ochre plasterwork is dwarfed by the Haj Manzil and Essel House to the left and the Delhi Stock Exchange to the right. A stock exchange needs no introduction but a Haj Manzil may. It's the place where Indian Muslims go to get their documentation processed before making the pilgrimage to Mecca. Every large

Walk
4

Turkman Gate

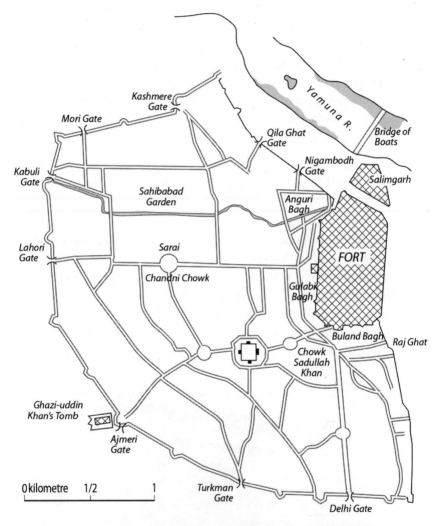

A Sketch Map of Shahjahanabad Showing the Main City Gates

Indian city has one and this is Delhi's. Yet, insignificant though the gate may look today, in the seventeenth century it was an impressive structure.

Shah Jahan transferred his capital to Delhi from Agra in 1638 and completed his city in 1649. There was an earlier perimeter wall of mud and stone but this wasn't strong enough so a second rubble wall was built and completed about 1658. The foundations of the second wall were dug to reach the level of the sub-soil water table to prevent an enemy from tunnelling underneath.

Historians say that Shah Jahan's walls served more to delineate the city boundary then defend it from attack, but even so the wall was 12 ft. thick and 27 ft. high. Now, only a little of it remains, and none here.

There are only a few of Shah Jahan's city gates left and this is one of them; the others are Ajmeri, Delhi, Nigambodh and Kashmere gates. Most of the city gates were exactly the same as the one you are looking at: square, pierced by high arches. The exceptions are Kashmere Gate with its double openings and Nigambodh Gate on the river bank which used to have a much lower arch than the others. It still does, but the gateway has been much altered over the years.

Walk
4
ॐ౷ॐ

In the seventeenth and eighteenth centuries, all the gates were closed at night and guards were posted.

As you stand facing the main arch of Turkman Gate, take the road (Faseel Road) which runs along the right-hand side of the gate itself and bends round to the right. You'll soon see a sign on the left-hand side of the road which reads: 'Holy Trinity Church'. Enter the courtyard.

Holy Trinity Church (Built 1905)

The doors of the church may be locked but someone will soon approach with a key to let you in if you tell them you are interested in seeing the inside. It seems to be usual here to take off your shoes before entering as you would in a mosque or temple. Although quite shady the interior is a surprise as it is so colourful. There are deep red arches behind the altar, a new shiny red floor and a light blue ceiling. With many vases of flowers in the church, you can see that it's a well-loved and beautifully cared for building that forms the centre of a lively Christian community. They have over 300 members.

The architectural style is solidly Byzantine and was built by the Cambridge Mission to serve local Christians.

Missionary work around Turkman Gate had been very active in the late nineteenth century as this district was one of the poorest and most crowded as it was occupied by the sweeper caste. This poverty was in stark contrast to the many grand mansions and great wealth in other parts of the city. The missionaries worked hard spreading the Gospel through preaching and good works. Some local residents did embrace Christianity, but on the whole the missionaries found both Muslims and Hindus tightly bound to their own faiths and difficult to convert. But there were exceptional times when famine affected Delhi and supplies of food from Christian missionary sources acted as a mighty persuader in creating conversions. However these new 'Christians' often returned to their former faiths when the lean years ended.

Leave the church and retrace your steps by walking back towards Turkman Gate.

Dargah of Hazrat Shah Turkman Bayabani (The Shrine of the Holy Man Turkman Bayabani)

Just before you reach the police station there is a shrine on your right under a tree, to the Muslim holy man Hazrat Shah Turkman Bayabani. This is the man who has given his name to the gate but whether or not this is his shrine is disputed. Most historians say it isn't the genuine one. However, the other is much harder to find so please content yourself with learning a little about him here. Despite its authenticity being argued over, Muslims regard the grave as a holy place and you see people entering to pray.

There's usually someone sitting inside or on the veranda keeping an eye on things.

Turkman Bayabani

Turkman Bayabani had built up a wide reputation as a man close to God and had been buried in this area long before Shah Jahan constructed his new city wall and gate in the 1650s. We know that Turkman Bayabani chose to live in the wilderness, as one of the names in his title (Bayabani) tells us that he belonged to a sect that preferred to worship Allah alone, rather than pray with others of his faith in a mosque.

Of the gate and the shrine, the holy man's shrine came first so that when the gate was built it took his name. Looking around at the busy urban character of Asif Ali Road today it's hard to believe that this area was ever wilderness and forest, but so it was. In the thirteenth century—which was Turkman Bayabani's time, the most inhabited area was 15 km to the south around the Qutab Minar.

Walk
4

The desperate need to earn a living has affected this little shrine. Turkman Bayabani's veranda now advertises 'ISD STD PCO Photo Stat' which operates from the narrowest of lanes just off to one side. There is sometimes a garland seller on the other half of the veranda.

Leave the shrine and walk past Turkman Gate Police Station, then the gate itself and turn right into the southern end of Sita Ram Bazaar which is here called Turkman Gate Main Bazaar. Before you turned you may have noticed the mosque ahead of you. It's most distinctive as it has an onion dome flanked by two ornate black and white minarets and is called Masjid Syed Faiz Ilahi. It's a large mosque used by pilgrims going on the Haj. They gather here as it is just opposite the Haj Manzil, the document centre for pilgrimages to Mecca, which I brought to your attention earlier.

Turkman Gate Main Bazaar

This is a tremendously chaotic street. Its shops, fruit barrows, cafes, donkey tethering area, rickshaws and motorbikes all tangle together and poor pedestrians are forced to dodge and weave for an inch of space.

Muzaffar Khan's Gateway

Keep walking along the left-hand side. You'll pass a large pink mosque that's being renovated—the Bari Masjid—and then come to some 1970s low-cost blocks of flats, easily seen behind an 'Al Saad Foods Shawarma Rolls' poster. Just a little further along on the left-hand side, opposite a chain shop (No. 1797), is an old nineteenth century archway. Stop in front of the archway. It used to belong to Muzaffar Khan, a wealthy Mughal noble, and was the entrance gateway to his haveli, or mansion. Now there's no trace of it except for this gateway with its symmetrical, much mutilated jharokas (the graceful, canopied windows), which you can see on either side of the gate. Today, these look like crumbling windows. The archway is locally known as 'Telion ka Phatak' or 'Gate of the Telis', as at one period a community of oil-extracting families settled around here obtaining the essence (tel) from flowers, vegetables and nuts, such as almonds. Today the arch houses a second-hand compressors business and is used as a store for old fridges and twin tubs.

It's said that Sharia law is partly responsible for there being so few mansions left in good condition in Old Delhi. According to Sharia law, every child gets a share of the property upon the father's death—unlike British law in which the eldest son traditionally got the lot! Sharia law can lead to properties becoming subdivided between many families and, if the children don't agree, to long-drawn-out legal battles and neglect.

Beads and Embroidery Accessories

Continue along Turkman Gate Bazaar Road and you'll notice that the shops have started selling beads. Millions of them in all shapes and sizes and made from every possible material. There are glass beads, brass, bone, ceramic, wooden and 'Chinee' with samples of each shop's speciality hanging across the open shop front. Most of the stock sits in dusty bags on high shelves. It's the same with the shops selling wholesale embroidery spangles and sequins, although in their case the goods are mostly in large glass jars. The street name has now changed to Main Road Kalan Mahal as we get nearer to the mosque, Kalan Masjid. For a glimpse into how we all cooked in the past, stop in front of Ghazali Enterprises, Shop No. 3002/2 on the left, and look across to an area painted mustard yellow where, through the gateway, you can see men cooking huge cauldrons of food over wooden fires. It's a party-catering enterprise specializing in Mughlai dishes. You could hire them for your next event!

Finding the Kalan Masjid

About fifty paces from the party caterer is the Kalan Masjid. To find it walk along on the right-hand side keeping an eye open for lanes on the left. The lane you want is behind a metal gate, usually open, which has an advertisement on the arch above for 'F Khan Physio Medi Care'. There's a bead shop (of course!) on the right—Shop No. 2919. You'll see the mosque at the top of a flight of steps. Climb up, take off your shoes and enter.

Kalan Masjid (Built 1387)

Because this mosque is so well-kept, often repainted and repaired, it doesn't look as old as it is. But it was here long before Shah Jahan built his capital city in the seventeenth century. Kalan Masjid was an important mosque in an earlier fourteenth century ruler's capital. The city at that time was called Ferozabad after its Sultan, Feroze Shah Tughluq. Although it doesn't seem a big mosque in comparison with the huge Jama Masjid opposite the Red Fort, its name 'Kalan' means large. It was a large mosque in fourteenth century Ferozabad. Locally, it is known as kali or black mosque because the outer walls were once of this colour.

Look at the cloisters, the prayer chamber opposite the entrance doorway, and the pulpit (minbar) next to the niche (mihrab) which indicates the direction of Mecca. This minbar has been clad with marble. Underneath is simple stone like that of the pillars. The rooms on either side of the main prayer chamber are for the use of women.

The man who built the Kalan Masjid was a senior minister in the court of Feroze Shah Tughluq for twenty years.

Finding Sultan Razia's Tomb in Bulbuli Khane

Descend the steps—you can rest on every fourth as they are made wider for this purpose—and turn left at the road. Continue for about another fifty paces along Kalan Masjid Main Bazaar road until you reach a fork in the road. On the house facing you is a poster that reads: 'Rehman & Sons'. You need to take the right-hand side of the fork to find Sultan Razia's tomb. To be doubly sure, you may look for Agate House. Take the road on the right opposite Agate House; another bead shop. Shopkeepers are used to directing people to Sultan Razia's tomb, so will wave you in the direction. Walk up the right-hand fork, then take the first road on the left. Turn left at—yes, another bead shop, and start walking uphill. Keep following this road as it climbs and you'll pass the Anis General Store. The lane makes many twists, but foreign visitors come here, so, as with the shopkeepers on Kalan Masjid Road the residents of these lanes will put you right if you go wrong. You'll come across plump goats and parked motorbikes, and as you near the tomb, a few workshops. There's a blue metal Archaeological Society of India sign (Protected Monument) at the tomb itself. The site is usually open as one half of it has become a mosque. The Archaeological Survey of India is still responsible for protecting the graves, and used to look after the whole site as an Ancient Monument. However, there was always a mihrab (prayer niche facing Mecca) in the west-facing wall and this has meant that people could argue that it was a mosque and that it shouldn't be closed to them. It's a contentious issue as the preservationists argue that the site will deteriorate in time if it is used so actively, especially as mosques always provide running water for ritual ablutions and this raises the water table.

Sultan Razia and Her Tomb

There's not much to see once you are there. The site itself is very simple, just two plain graves in an open mausoleum. It's finding them that's fun.

Books vary in their use of Sultan or Sultana to describe Razia. A Sultan is a Muslim sovereign whereas a Sultana is the mother, wife, daughter, or in rare cases, concubine of a Sultan. By birth Razia was a Sultana but through force of personality became a Sultan. She ruled from her fortress palace near the Qutub Minar.

Her story is a sad one. Her father was the strong and important Sultan of Delhi Shams-ud-din-Iltutmish. On his death his son became Sultan, but as the nobles disliked him, they revolted, forcing him to fight them. Consequently, they later killed him and his mother, whom they also disliked.

While all this was going on, his sister Razia took over the Sultanate of Delhi as she had popular support from the local nobility and the common people. She ruled successfully for three years, but her life was one long power struggle against her provincial nobility who felt that choosing the Sultan was their prerogative. Eventually, while out of Delhi, subduing a rebel fort, she was captured and imprisoned. She made what she hoped would be a politically useful union—she married her captor. The two of them tried to regain the Sultanate but their plans failed and they fled.

Some say she was killed in battle, others that she was murdered by robbers whilst resting under a tree. The place of her death isn't known precisely. She was probably brought to this present spot for

Walk
4

burial because it was near to the grave of the holy man Turkman Bayabani. Sultan Razia was one of his followers.

The grave next to Razia's is said to be that of her sister Saziya, about whom absolutely nothing is known.

Retrace your twists and turns to Kalan Masjid Road—you must always be going downhill. Once on the main road if you need to get your bearings again find the Agate House bead shop and with your back to it walk left. This time you're taking the left-hand fork. Continue walking along the main thoroughfare which has now morphed into the well-known old shopping street Sita Ram Bazaar. You can check the name of the street on the shop signs and keep an eye on the shop numbers. You don't turn off until Shop No. 972.

Finding Kucha Pati Ram

This kucha is almost at the end of this long road so you have to walk at least 700 metres before you get near it. (Consult your map.) You'll pass an amazing variety of shops, little grocery stores, paan sellers, fruit and vegetable barrows and the odd bangle shop. It's a fascinating walk. The entrance to Kucha Pati Ram is on the left-hand side, narrow and unimpressive. You need to turn left at Shop No. 972: K K Industries (aluminium door handles) which often has a lemon seller on the pavement in front of it. This is the lane you want. As another check there's a fancy three-storey house, painted a pale mauve, on the right-hand corner of the lane with an ornately carved and curvy second-storey balcony. However, this is a very well-known street, so check by repeating the name of the Kucha you want—Pati Ram—whilst pointing hopefully at a lane, to any local shopkeeper and he'll put you right. Turn into Kucha Pati Ram.

Kucha Pati Ram

This lane is still partly residential although it is fast becoming just another business street. Catch the remaining doorways before they disappear! Yet, you still can wander along admiring the craftsmanship of some of the house fronts. They are early or late nineteenth and early twentieth century but the styles echo those of earlier centuries and give you an idea of what a prosperous nineteenth century Old Delhi ·residential street used to be like.

At the beginning of the Kucha on the right, there is often an open gateway allowing you to see into a pleasant courtyard with brightly painted doors and plants in pots. You'll soon come to a large plain grand house with a sign 'Sri Ram Barrister at Law'. I wonder if he still lives there? Look at the house a little further down on the opposite side. It has the most amazingly ornate miniature balconies and carvings of Hindu characters over the doorway. The figure in the middle is a depiction of Dhruv, a follower of Lord Vishnu, supported on either side by decorative buxom ladies. Continue to enjoy the doorways as you walk down the street. You'll pass a large Hindu temple opposite a sign on the left for 'The Saria Clinic'.

One doorway just off Kucha Pati Ram is worth finding. It's a particularly grand doorway with three small peacocks at the apex of the arch. It's in a side street on the left just opposite Shop No. 601 Kucha Pati Ram (Manak Antique Gift Gallery). Peacocks were always well-liked by craftsmen but after Shah Jahan had so magnificently incorporated this beautiful bird into his Peacock Throne their popularity was given an even greater boost.

Return to Kucha Pati Ram and follow the road round to the right. The route takes you through what once was a chowk or a square, though now it has become more of a triangle, encroached upon by a Hindu shrine and motorbike repair workshops. Follow the route further through a second square (chowk), now also made much smaller as it contains an·electricity substation in its midst. With your back to the substation, keep right, and as you approach the Ajmeri Gate area you will notice that the shops start selling pipes and tubes while the name of the street changes to Gali Kunde Walen. Soon you come to the Ajmeri Gate Road and

Walk
4
෨෮

if you look left the bulk of Ajmeri Gate itself is easily seen ahead. You are now in the heart of wholesale plumbing and hardware and this road is always incredibly busy.

Your walk ends here unless you have obtained permission to enter the madrasa and tomb of Ghazi-uddin in the Anglo Arabic Senior Secondary School. The school itself starts at 8 a.m. and closes at 2 p.m. Take a cycle or scooter rickshaw back to your car or to the nearest Metro station, which is at New Delhi Railway Station.

The Madrasa and Tomb of Ghazi-uddin

If you have obtained permission, look across the wide crowded road to the trees opposite and you'll see an old red sandstone building amongst them. This is the madrasa. Keep to the right-hand side of Ajmeri Gate and negotiate the chaos of Shraddhanand Marg. (This wide road coming in from the right is the centre of Delhi's red light area where prostitutes are still referred to as 'dancing girls'. It used to be called Garstin Bastion Road and is still often referred to as G.B. Road in reports in the local papers (especially when there have been 'mishaps' and murders, with culprits 'absconding'.) Make for the sign you can see in the distance—'Anglo Arabic Sr. Secondary School' written in English and Urdu. This isn't above the main gate itself so with your back to the main road walk left and after a few metres you'll come to the main gate. Show the security guard your letter and he will let you in.

The Madrasa of Ghazi-uddin (1692)

It's such a lovely sight; the neat garden, the pale white domes of the mosque, the trees, and the tranquillity after the anarchy of the road outside. Cross to the left-hand corner of the courtyard, climb four steps and walk towards a set of pierced stone screens. Take off your shoes and climb a few more steps, so that you are parallel with the mosque, and look at the tomb of the man who built

The Tomb of Ghazi-uddin Bahadur Firoz Jang

the madrasa. The tomb of Ghazi-uddin Khan—who was given the title of Firoz Jang—is quite simple, but a very good example of seventeenth century pierced screen work. You'll see more than one grave; Ghazi-uddin's is the one in the middle. There are some heartbreakingly tiny graves just outside the main tomb. Some of the original panels became broken and have been replaced.

The man, Ghazi-uddin, was an extremely successful and highly respected military commander in Aurangzeb's army. Time and again his wits and loyalty were tested and never found lacking. In 1689 he caught the plague and it left him blind, but even sightless he was so esteemed that Aurangzeb asked his advice on military matters.

After Aurangzeb's death Ghazi-uddin was appointed Governor of Gujarat and he died there. His body was brought back to the tomb he'd already built and the madrasa that bore his name.

It was common for Mughal noblemen to want their tombs to be an integral part of a centre of learning. Islam places a very high value on literacy, as members of the faith are expected to be able to read the Koran. So, setting up a centre of learning was a prestigious way of continuing the fame of your own noble name after your death and, you hoped, of gaining spiritual merit. Two other well-known tombs in Delhi which had madrasas attached to them at one time are Humayun's tomb and Safdarjang's tomb.

Built at the end of the seventeenth century, the madrasa remained as Ghazi-uddin would have known it throughout the eighteenth century. It was a school where Arabic and the traditional sciences were taught in Persian, the language of the Mughal court.

You can still see the form of the old madrasa very clearly. On either side of the courtyard are two tiers of five small rooms or cells.

There used to be a large water tank in front of the mosque but this was filled in by a British Principal in the nineteenth century.

In 1824, the old madrasa was repaired and renamed Delhi College. This college had a tremendous influence on the life of the city because its teachers were so highly esteemed. In the 1830s and 1840s, it became the centre of a rich scientific and literary-cultural flowering known as the Delhi Renaissance. During this period, traditional Oriental learning and Western ideas met and enriched each other. There were very popular poetry evenings held in the grounds—so popular that Ajmeri Gate had to be kept open later than usual to allow people back into the city after the readings had finished. The language of this cultural outburst was Urdu, a blending of Hindi and Persian.

It all came to an end with the Uprising in 1857. The British authorities never allowed the college to regain its former prestige as a centre of university-level learning, in spite of an appeal from local citizens and local funds being available.

It was renamed Zakir Husain College after a minister in Nehru's government. It is now the Anglo Arabic Senior Secondary School and a co-ed, secular institution. After 350 years of being a boys' school, girls were admitted in 2012.

Walk
4

Your walk ends here.

Take an auto or cycle rickshaw back to your car or to the nearest Metro station—which from here is New Delhi Metro Station. Taxis are also available from the station.

Walk 5:
Busy Market Streets

A walk for the nimble through one of Old Delhi's busiest thoroughfares south of the Jama Masjid. The roads in this walk are usually extremely congested for most of their length so walkers who dislike crowds and noise should beware. It is a pungent morning, afternoon or evening walk on any day and a possible Sunday walk, although on a Sunday there's a very busy market on the pavement along Netaji Subhash Road which makes the approach more difficult. If you wish to see the vegetable market at its busiest, start your walk very early in the morning. All the streets are lined with shops and often have vegetable stalls in front of them. This is why you need to be nimble to dodge between the many pedestrians, stalls, rickshaws and motorbikes. This is a walk simply to absorb the feel of an old established Muslim area. There aren't any major buildings to visit so it can be completed quickly if you charge along. However it's best appreciated slowly as it gives insights into a different way of life to that which most of us know. Warning: This walk takes you past poultry shops and goat-butchers' shops so there is blood on the ground and this attracts flies.

Places of Interest
    KASTURBA GANDHI MARG
    POULTRY SELLERS
    BAZAAR MATYA MAHAL

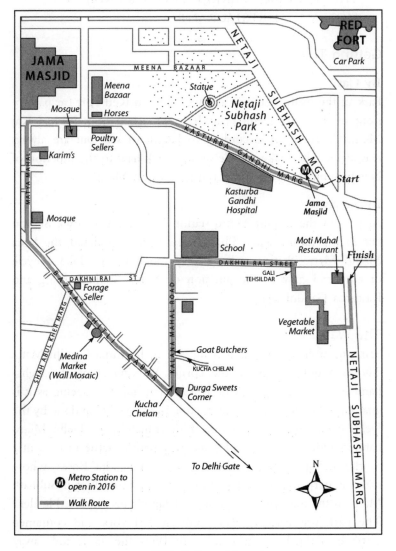

Walk 5: Route Map

CHITLI QABAR BAZAAR
KALAN MAHAL
THE VEGETABLE MARKET (PHOOL MANDI)
MOTI MAHAL RESTAURANT

Getting There

By Car

Park in the well-organized and well-known Red Fort car park in front of the fort's Delhi Gate. It's approached from Nishad Raj Marg. Charges vary according to length of stay but are always reasonable. Then take a cycle or auto rickshaw to the junction of Netaji Subhash Marg and Kasturba Gandhi Marg.

By Metro

At present the nearest Metro station is Chandni Chowk Station but in the future, when Phase 3 has been completed, the Jama Masjid Metro Station will be very much nearer. Take a cycle or auto rickshaw to the junction of Netaji Subhash Marg and Kasturba Gandhi Marg.

Walk
5

The Walk

Start the walk on the right-hand side of Kasturba Gandhi Marg. There's a police post on the corner. Walking along the right-hand side is better at present as it's much quieter—seeing as it is guarded by police who are protecting the work being done by the Delhi Metro Rail Corporation. Unfortunately, the Delhi Metro barriers hide what was a pleasant park with a statue in its centre to the Indian nationalist hero Subhash Chandra Bose—whose name is perpetuated in a slightly different form, Netaji Subhash Marg, in the road you've just left. (Netaji means respected leader.) The park was formerly King Edward VII Park and contained a statue of the king on a horse. In 1969, the statue rode away, with help from respective governments, to Queen's Park, Toronto where it can still be found. Although you can't see the present statue of Subhash Chandra Bose for the barriers, he's so important he's worth knowing something about, so take a minute to read about his life.

Subhash Chandra Bose

He was a nationalist politician who had an aggressive approach to getting rid of the British, which was in complete opposition to Gandhi's peaceful style of non-cooperation. After World War 2 began and Indian troops were fighting for the Allies in their millions, Bose left India for Berlin. He believed 'the enemies of my enemies are my friends' and tried to get support from Nazi Germany. It wasn't forthcoming so he went to Japan. Here he was successful. He formed the Indian National Army from Indian prisoners-of-war held by the Japanese. They had some success fighting alongside the Japanese in Burma with the battle cry 'Jai Hind', (Victory to India). Later, however, they had to retreat. For, after Hiroshima, Japan surrendered and the INA did too.

Walk
5
ঙ৩৺৩৺

The Statue of Subhash Chandra Bose

Continue walking along this road and after about 150 metres look over to the left-hand side. You'll soon see signs such as New OPD Block (Out Patients Department) and then about 50 metres further along you'll see the main gate with its large 'Kasturba Gandhi Hospital' sign in Hindi and English. Cross over to the hospital.

Kasturba Gandhi Hospital (Named after Mahatma Gandhi's Wife)

This is a free women's and children's hospital run by North Delhi Municipal Corporation. Between fifteen and twenty babies are born in this hospital every day. There are a lot of snack stands around the main gate catering to visitors and the relatives of the patients—especially the ones waiting for news of a baby's arrival. Relatives can stay inside the hospital itself in a designated 'Relative Waiting Room' or temporarily camp out under metal sheeting inside the railings themselves. You may see husbands dropping off their heavily pregnant wives, going off to park and then returning. It's most appropriate that a women's hospital is named after Kasturba Gandhi as at one time as well as teaching reading and writing, she also taught hygiene.

This hospital didn't start life named after Gandhi's wife. It was started in 1905 by a Lady Milton and had ten beds. Five years later it was named after Queen Victoria. It became the Victoria Zenana (Women's) Hospital. By 1975, it had grown to 450 beds and was renamed the Kasturba Gandhi Hospital in honour of Mahatma Gandhi's wife. It's a more sophisticated hospital now with eight departments, an emergency service, a blood bank and its own school of nursing. For years it was known locally as 'machli walon ka aspital' or, 'the fish-sellers' hospital', as it was very near the wholesale fish market!

Continue walking along Kasturba Gandhi Marg.

The Fish Market in the 1980s

Poultry Sellers and Mosquito Netting

You'll come across the poultry sellers on the left-hand side of the road about 150 metres from the hospital. They start just after you cross a road on the left. The caged hens, often crowded together, look in a miserable condition; the beautiful cockerels have a better life as they strut above the cages. As well as live birds you'll see them being dressed; sometimes being plucked or having their heads and feet chopped off. After some 50 metres you'll notice the three mosquito netting sellers; there's one on the left with his wares hanging from a structure really intended to carry electricity cables. These nets look very like fishermen's nets as they are weighted along the bottom edge with small brown lengths of tubing. The net sellers will delicately repair old torn mosquito netting if asked.

Two White Horses

.Walk
5
ঙ৹৩৳

Surprisingly, there are stables along this road. To see them, stop on the left-hand side of Kasturba Gandhi Marg when you reach two shops: Chicken Bite and Central Poultry Chicken and Fish Shop. Look across the road and you'll see a large iron gate with spikes on the top which has a smaller gate within it leading down to the Meena Bazaar. There are often cars parked in front of this gate so it's easy to miss. Cross over to the gate and you'll see on your left outside the gate a slightly plump white horse called Moti (Fatty) and one with slender ankles called Piel (ankle bracelet). They are hired by grooms to ride on their wedding day or for other ceremonial purposes. They're kept fit; they have a canter around Old Delhi twice a day.

Cross back to the left-hand side and look up. Above the shops are pilgrimage hotels and at ground level, many cafes such as Kashmiri Zaiqa. As well as the locals, they cater to visitors coming to the mosque from outside the Delhi area. You may notice Muslim men, identifiable by their very red beards (in honour of the prophet), dressed differently from Delhi men as they may have come in from Haryana or Bihar. This is particularly true during the times of Muslim festivals. The shops cater to their need to take home gifts for the family too, such as religious cassettes, prayer mats, books, souvenir clocks and fancy packets of dates and sweets. Keep walking until you are opposite Gate 1 of the Jama Masjid. You'll see a road with Yaseen Hotel on the left-hand corner. Turn left into it. You have arrived at Matya Mahal.

Matya Mahal (The Earth-Coloured Palace)

The palace, or large house, isn't here anymore. Much has taken its place! Immediately on your left is a large shop selling Indian sweets such as barfi, gulab jamuns and lassi in rustic earthenware 'glasses'. There are several well-known restaurants near the entrance to Matya Mahal, the most famous being Karim's. It's on the left, down the first alley, just a few steps past the New Jawahar Restaurant which is also recommended as it has an air-conditioned room at the top. It's easy to miss Karim's if you're not careful, as it is at the bottom of the alley. If you look down you'll see the name 'Karim's' on a sign, above cooks stirring huge cauldrons of mutton korma or curry sauces with men behind tossing romali roti into the air. It opens at 6 a.m. and closes at midnight. It's famous for its Mughal cuisine. The food is generally rich; buttery sauces are a specialty, and the naan is fresh, hot and delicious. The service is good, as there are many waiters and table clearers, and you never have long to wait for your meal. Nowadays there are branches of this restaurant in the outlying areas of Noida, Gurgaon, Greater Kailash, Green Park and Malviya Nagar. Seeing as it's a Muslim restaurant they don't serve alcohol, so a quick cold drink has to be a soft one.

This doesn't happen at Karim's. They keep their courtyard free, but as you walk along Matya Mahal you'll come across very poor people sitting in orderly rows outside some of the restaurants such as Rehmatullah Hotel and Ghareeb Nawaz Hotel. ('Hotel' here implies restaurant.) They're waiting for the generous, often

Walk
5
ക്ലൗൽ

religious-minded diners to buy them a simple meal of two rotis and a dollop of vegetables. You can feed about three or four men for 100 rupees. Just pass over some notes and the chief cook will decide how many get free food.

Islam is always encouraging its followers to feed the poor and you are supposed to give the food to the men personally. However, others will do it for you if you leave a donation with the man at the cash desk. It's always most gratefully received.

You can easily tell you're in a Muslim area of the city as you walk along Bazaar Matya Mahal. Many of the women are wearing a long, plain black coat (burqa), although on younger women fashionable sparkly decorations have crept in on cuffs and edgings. Most of the men are wearing Islamic skull caps, or topis.

Walk
5
ॐॐ

There's a lot of Urdu on shop signs and the shops themselves differ from those on Chandni Chowk. The cloth shops stock greater varieties of brocades and velvets liked by Muslim women (under the burqas) and you see men making naan, or roomali roti, the very thin round bread cooked on a hot upturned dome, far more frequently than chappatis. The butchers, with their goat carcasses hanging from hooks, are of course all halal. Halal means 'permitted' or 'lawful' and is food that a Muslim can safely eat without breaking any of their strict dietary rules. It does not contain any alcohol or food products from forbidden animals, such as pigs, and a prayer dedicating the slaughter to Allah is recited over each animal before it is killed. There are many, many mosques in the area. You'll walk past several and see the minarets of others if you look down the side streets.

The road name on the shops is Matya Mahal to begin with, but after walking about 500 metres you may notice that the name of this road changes once you've passed a busy junction where roads come in at an angle from both left and right and form a small ragged intersection. On the shops the name changes to a chowk or square, but it isn't really a square. (Technically, in English I'm told, it's an off-set junction.) There's a bakery sign for 'New

Janta Bakery, Matya Mahal Chowk, Dujanan House' above an end shop next to Nice Purse Corner on the road coming in from the right. You will need to take the left-hand fork. Opposite this, on the left, is a man who sells forage for goats, so walk past him. He's always got piles of branches full of leaves so his shop makes a bright green landmark especially in the morning when his fresh stock has just arrived. One last check is that there's a multi-storey white painted building facing you at the fork which is Hotel Shezan although you'll only see the sign once you've taken the left-hand fork. From here onwards you're in an extension of Matya Mahal which is known as Chitli Qabar.

Chitli Qabar (Holy Man Chitli's Grave)

You have to walk along Chitli Qabar for about a quarter of a mile, so do so slowly, absorbing the detail of everyday life around you. Walk down the left side of the road as there's a modern, green, fancy cusped marble archway with white stars down the front of green fluted pillars, about a 100 meters from the junction of roads you've just left. It's next to Shop No. 1361, Nazim Ali's Hush Textile shop. The fancy arch is on the right-hand side, but you can see it better from the left. Today, it marks the entrance to Medina Market, a shopping cul-de-sac specializing in textiles. On the right-hand side of the arch is something that will surprise you; a large, attractive mosaic of the Prophet's Mosque in Medina, Saudi Arabia. The shopkeepers clubbed together to have it installed in 2010. Yet this modern archway replaces a much older one. It used to mark the entrance to a nobleman's house. He was Nawab Kallu Khawas. Unfortunately, his beautiful house has disappeared. This area saw a massive population change after partition in 1947. The Muslim descendants of the Nawab left this property to move to Pakistan and homeless Hindu families were originally settled here in the '40s by the Indian government. This pattern was repeated time and time again and goes some way in explaining why there are so few havelis (mansions) in good condition left in

Shahjahanabad when at one time there were so many.

Finding Kuche Fouad Khan

Continue walking along Chitli Qabar Bazaar for about 200 metres. You leave it by turning left into a side street named Kuche Fouad Khan. Don't worry too much about counting side streets, as Kuche Fouad Khan has shops called Durga Sweets on both sides of the narrow turning that you want, which can serve as an effective check. Although the two shops share a name, they are in essence quite different; Durga Sweets on the right-hand side sells typical Indian sweets such as barfi and laddus, whereas Durga Sweets on the left is more of a savoury snackbar selling fried samosas. A famous Kucha called Kucha Chelan leads off on the right from Kuche Fouad Khan quite near the entrance, but don't go down it! Keep walking straight ahead as Kuche Fouad Khan becomes Kalan Mahal.

Walk
5

Kalan Mahal (Big Palace)

Continue along this street, packed to capacity with a wide variety of shops: grocers, vegetable stalls, street food sellers, electrical goods, tailors, barbers, and interspersed between them all—goat butchers. Some sell the meat, others specialize in hooves, while others can be seen skinning goats' heads; it's all a far cry from buying a few chops in a polystyrene tray from Sainsbury's. As you get further into the kuche, check the name of the street on the shop signs and you'll see that it changes to Kalan Mahal.

The next landmark you need to look out for is about 150 metres ahead on the right. You must turn right here. (Consult your map.) It's a 10-ft. high white plaster wall topped by metal railings and divided up by sandstone columns. It's on your right and you turn right here. It surrounds a school. Another sign that you've reached the right spot is a huge tangle of cables crossing the road from a very tall telegraph pole—while on the left are a few little shops painted blue.

Turn right here and walk along with the school wall on your left. To begin with, the road name doesn't change but it will very soon! You can see the lane's name beneath Kitab Bhavan—1284 Kalan Mahal.

The government school that you see here is Sarvodaya Bal Vidyalaya and as you pass an entrance gateway you'll see it proudly proclaim a midday meal scheme. Soon, the same street changes its name to Kuche Dakhni Rai. Another 100 metres further along on the right there's a gate with a cross above it and the words 'Christian Colony' on a signboard. This gate leads into a block of pleasant flats which are home to about twenty-five Protestant and Roman Catholic families. They were built over a hundred years ago by Reverend King. Many of the Protestant families worship at Delhi's oldest Christian church, St James', near Kashmere Gate. The residents of this colony are worried at present as the diocese has sold the property; their future, therefore, is uncertain. In future years the cross on the wall and the signboard may have disappeared.

Walk
5
ਰਓਿਓਖ਼

The Walk to the Vegetable Market

To get to the vegetable market you need to turn right off Kalan Mahal down a road called Gali Tehsildar. Keep walking along Kalan Mahal until you see a road coming in from the right. There's a shop called Rozana on the left and a cement shop on the right, Alfa Cement. Turn right here and walk along Gali Tehsildar. Immediately after following the road, sharp left, you come to a Y junction. Turn left at the junction. Then take the second very narrow alley on your right. On one side is a brick wall and on the other a dark rather sunken cafe serving tea and snacks to men working in the vegetable market. This alley will lead you into the wholesale vegetable market. It may seem blocked by sacks of potatoes and you can only get round them on the left-hand side.

Phool Mandi (The Flower Market)
[In Reality a Wholesale Vegetable Market]

Wholesale flowers have gone, with the fish and poultry, out to Ghazipur. Vegetables rule! It's an incredibly busy place from 3 a.m. to 10 a.m. but after that it slackens off. It starts again at 8 p.m. when lorries start arriving to unload their fresh supplies.

The wholesalers have warehouses all around the market square for piling up the sacks of potatoes, onions, cabbages and cauliflowers and the ground is slippery with discarded leaves which the goats eat up. They even eat potatoes but one small spud takes a lot of chewing!

There are many porters working here, most 'tied' to a particular wholesaler, but some are freelance and on good days can earn much more than their 'tied' colleagues.

Vegetables arrive from all over the place. Uttar Pradesh sends potatoes, onions, garlic, and green vegetables, as does Haryana; Rajasthan supplies hundreds of kilos of tomatoes. From here they're distributed throughout Delhi. In summer there is a lot of sugarcane too. Leave the market by picking your way carefully across the square (the old cobbles can be slippery), then take the narrow central lane out into the main street which is Netaji Subhash Marg. Turn left and walk along for a few metres until you reach the Moti Mahal Restaurant.

Walk
5
ॐ✿ॐ

Moti Mahal (Pearl Palace) Restaurant

This restaurant is very well-known because it was the first in Delhi to offer meat and fish cooked in a tandoor—a clay oven. Tandoori cooking traditionally belongs to the north-west frontier of India and the family that started Moti Mahal were refugees from this area who came to Delhi after the partition of India. It started life as a small restaurant but became so popular that it grew. Even though ownership has changed hands, the style of cooking hasn't. Succulent tandoori dishes still dominate the menu. Gordon Ramsay, the famously foul-mouthed British chef, was taught to cook butter chicken here! The restaurant has photos to prove it.

Every night from about 8 p.m. to 11.00 p.m., customers can listen to artistes singing qawallis and gazals, and songs from Hindi films. The restaurant is closed on Tuesdays. On other days it's open from noon to midnight. The restaurant doesn't serve alcohol.

Your walk ends here.

Enter for a drink and a snack or take a cycle or auto rickshaw back to your car at the Red Fort's Delhi Gate or to a Metro station. New Delhi Metro Station would be the nearest from here.

Walk
5
ॐ

Walk **6:**
Spices, Nuts and Pickles

Sacks of spices and chillies, sheets of silver, an old mosque, and tales from Delhi's past. An aromatic weekday walk for mornings, beginning at about 9.30 a.m. In the afternoons and evenings this area is extremely busy. Although the Wholesale Spice Market (Gadodia), is closed on Sundays many of the shops themselves are open so it is possible to do the walk on a Sunday. If you can, avoid Khari Baoli altogether during the run up to Diwali as the street is unbelievably crowded. This is one of the shorter walks.

Places of Interest
    KHARI BAOLI'S NUTS, SPICES, AND PICKLE SHOPS
    THE WHOLESALE SPICE MARKET (GADODIA MARKET)
    THE FATEHPURI MOSQUE
    HAIDER QULI KHAN'S GATEWAY
    LALA CHUNNA MAL'S HAVELI

Getting There

By Car
Park in the large, well-known and well-organized Red Fort car park in front of the fort's Delhi gate. It's approached from Nishad Raj Marg. Charges vary according to length of stay but are always reasonable. It's open from 8 a.m. to 10 p.m. Then get an auto or cycle rickshaw to the start of your walk at the Chandni Chowk

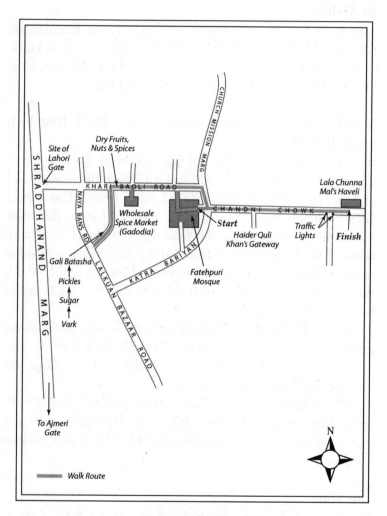

Walk 6: Route Map

entrance to the Fatehpuri Mosque. It's at the opposite end of the street from the Red Fort.

By Metro

Take the Yellow Line for Chandni Chowk station. Exit through Gate 5 and walk to Chandni Chowk itself. Take a cycle rickshaw to the Chandni Chowk entrance of the Fatehpuri Mosque. It's at the opposite end of the street from the Red Fort.

Background Information about Khari Baoli (Brackish Stepped Well)

It's a very busy street today and was important in Shah Jahan's time too. There used to be a fortified gateway at the westerly end of Khari Baoli, through which a road led to Lahore. This 'Lahori Gate' no longer exists. As well as the route to Lahore, this street had another claim to fame. 300 years ago, one branch of a canal, bringing fresh water from a point on the river Yamuna 75 miles north of here, entered the city and ran along the centre of this street. The canal turned right at the end of Khari Baoli before flowing along Chandni Chowk itself.

Walk
6
ॐ॰ॐ

The canal provided water for the city people, its trees and gardens, before being channelled into the Red Fort to run between gem-studded marble pillars under golden ceilings and through hundreds of silver fountains.

The stepped well called Khari Baoli predates Shah Jahan's seventeenth century city. It was dug in the sixteenth century and may be hidden inside a building somewhere but it isn't obvious any more.

The Walk

Although you've been dropped off at the Chandni Chowk entrance to the mosque, don't enter immediately as you'll be calling in on your way back. You'll really appreciate its calmness after the hurly burly of Khari Baoli.

Walk 1: Red Fort: Hall of Public Audience

Walk 1: Red Fort: Curtain Wall; Early Morning

Walk 1: Red Fort: Terrace Pavilion

Walk 1: Red Fort: Private Palace; Screen

Walk 2: Jama Masjid: Courtyard

Walk 2: Meena Bazaar Road: Prayer Mats

Walk 2: Nai Sarak: Wedding Veils

Walk 2: Chawri Bazaar: End of the School Day

Walk 3: Naughara: Jain Temple Ceiling

Walk 3: Naughara: Nineteenth-century Doorways

Walk 3: Kinari Bazaar: Wedding Street Braid Seller.

Walk 4: Sitaram Bazaar: Bead Shop

Walk 4: Kalan Mahal: with Mouse

Walk 4: Kalan Mahal: Entrance

Walk 5: Vegetable Market: Before Dawn

Walk 5: Vegetable Market: Wholesale Tomatoes

Walk 5: Kasturba Gandhi Marg: Wedding Horses

Walk 6: Khari Baoli Road

Walk 6: Spice Market: Chillies

Walk 6: Spice Market: Courtyard Architecture

Walk 7: Chandni Chowk from Lajpat Rai Market

Walk 7: Bankhandi: Holy Baba Temple

Walk 7: Delhi (Main) Railway Station

Walk 7: Delhi (Main) Railway Station: Platform Scene

Walk 8: Chandni Chowk: Jain and Hindu Temples

Walk 8: Chandni Chowk: Garland Stall

Walk 8: Sisganj Gurdwara: Courtyard Scene

Walk 9: Lothian Road: St James' Church

Walk 9: Lothian Road: Pavement Dwellers

Walk 9: Lothian Road: Telegraph Memorial

Walk 10: Qudsia Bagh: Open Air Meeting

Walk 10: Shamnath Marg: Maidens Hotel

The Spices and Nuts on Khari Baoli Road

With your back to the entrance turn left; you'll see A1 Dry Fruit Store on your left as you continue walking along the pavement passing lots of small shops piled high with nuts, raisins, and spices for about 60 metres. The pavement bends round to the left at the junction of the road you're walking along, Katra Baryan, with Khari Baoli Road. Fortunately, there is usually a foot or two of space left for pedestrians between the shops themselves and the pavement sellers on the edge of the kerb! Just after the bend you'll see the flashing neon sign of Ram Bhandar's nut shop and a few metres further along, pass the Khari Baoli entrance to the Fatehpuri Mosque. You'll return to this entrance later.

The shops are both retail and wholesale. The retail prices are stuck into the sacks. To obtain wholesale prices you have to buy very large quantities, for example over 55 kilos of raisins, 75 kilos of almonds or 100 kilos of sugar—but small packets are available. The nuts and dried fruits are so attractive you may want to buy here, especially as Khari Baoli goods have a reputation for being the best in Delhi. If you see a spice you don't recognize, refer to the 'Spices Reference Section' at the end of this walk.

Continue walking along on the left, passing even more fruit and spice shops, for about another 70 metres and then when you come to a lane which leads under a covered archway, turn left. You'll have reached the Wholesale Spice Market. As a check, the shops on either side are Haveli Ram Mulkan Raj on the left and on the right, Shop No. 1 of Gadodia Market: Shudh Masala which advertises that they 'Deal in All type Snuff'.

The Wholesale Spice Market (Gadodia)

Look up at the fancy wrought iron work at the apex of the arch. It incorporates the name Gadodia, but at present the name is partly masked by a dusty poster saying 'No Photography without Permission' which is universally ignored. The market was built about eighty-five years ago (in the 1920s) by a merchant, Seth

Gadodia Market, Khari Baoli

Lakshmi Narayan Gadodia, and that is why it bears his name. Enter the covered arcade and it will lead you into an open square lined on all sides with wholesale spice dealers' storerooms. Large weighing scales take pride of place at the front of each. Unfortunately, the centre of the courtyard has been built on and so the spaciousness of the original design has disappeared. There's just a narrow channel around the wholesalers' shops now.

Yet it is still an interesting square, as the three storeys of offices and flats above the wholesalers are brightly painted and ornately decorated. It's a pity it's becoming rather ramshackle.

Between 10 a.m. and noon, this area is sometimes so congested—with porters struggling to get their long barrows piled high with sacks to the wholesalers—that it's impossible to walk around. However, if the way looks clear, circumnavigate the courtyard and see the different sizes and qualities of chillies, turmeric, aniseed, dried mango, black salt, tamarind, and cloves. There's even a product that looks like dried moss. It's called charila and is collected from the banks of rivers and added to sauces to intensify the flavour. The open sacks of red chillies are wonderfully photogenic. The air in the courtyard is so full of spices that you often leave the market sneezing. Return to Khari Baoli.

Pickles, Chutneys and Murabba

Many of the spice shops also sell pickles, chutneys and murabba. Pickles are sour and hot. Chutneys are sweet and sour. The mixed pickle is the most popular with Delhi people, according to the shopkeepers. Mango pickle is one of the hottest of the commercially produced pickles, while the lemon pickle is a mild but distinctively bitter product.

Murabba refers to fruit preserved in sugar. There's a wide range available: cherries, apples, Indian gooseberries (amla), pineapples, chopped peel, even preserved carrots which are the cheapest. Preserves are mostly eaten in the cooler months—except for Indian gooseberries which are eaten all the year round. They aren't served as a pudding course but with a savoury meal, the way apple sauce is served with pork in Britain.

The Walk to Gali Batashan for Vark (Edible Silver)

If you'd like to buy edible silver leaves (vark) to give a Mughal touch to a special dish, then stay on the left and walk a further 150 metres until you reach a sloping lane coming in from the left. It's protected from cars entering it by a motley assortment of metal girders and stone bollards—five in all—which do stop cars but aren't wide enough to stop the scourge of motorbikes. The shop on the left is the Delhi Jam House (a general store), while on the right stands Harnarains (a large dried fruit shop).

Stop at the second shop on the left in Gali Batashan, immediately after Delhi Jam. Its name is Shrinath and Co, and is a party products shop which sells paper plates and cups and vark in small white packs. The edible silver is sandwiched between pieces of thin white paper. You can buy vark over the internet but it is much cheaper do so here, which, according to the shop owner is 100 per cent pure. However, you must check. To ensure that any vark you buy is 100 per cent pure, test it with a match. If you set fire to it and it splutters it isn't pure. Don't handle the vark itself; let it fall gently onto the top of your dish. It can add a very special sparkle!

Turn round here and retrace your steps as you are now walking back up Khari Baoli towards the Fatehpuri Mosque, the entrance to which you passed earlier. It's on your right about 200 metres from Gali Batashan.

The Fatehpuri Mosque (Built 1650)

Take off your shoes and carry them, soles together, into the mosque as there isn't always anyone to take care of them. Walk into the courtyard and enjoy the peacefulness of this sacred place.

This mosque was built by a noble lady, Fatehpuri Begum,

Walk
6
ॐ☸

one of Shah Jahan's wives, and dominated the western end of the important thoroughfare of Chandni Chowk.

Walk into the courtyard and stand behind the pool facing the central dome. Look at the pipe on the left-hand side of the pool from which water is constantly pouring. It is used for Islamic ritual ablutions, which must be carried out in running water. In the left-hand corner of the courtyard is a row of taps providing water for washing clothes or other everyday uses.

Walk up to the prayer hall, the covered area of the mosque, and look at the back wall. In the middle is a large central niche, the mihrab, which points to Mecca. The Koranic extract, written in Arabic, is simple yet striking. Once you've finished exploring the prayer hall return to the mihrab and turn round so that you're facing a carved stone platform which has a small white metal stepladder to its top. This is a dikka (mihrab and dikka have been explained in Walk 4). It is used as a platform for a man whose job it is to keep the people praying in the courtyard in touch with the Imam's (prayer leader's) activities in the hall. Sitting on top, he is a human amplifier as he chants in unison with the Imam, and copies the Imam's changing postures as well. The dikka is used on Fridays and festival days.

Walk into the centre of the courtyard and face the clock over the Chandni Chowk gateway. Look at the walls around the courtyard. On your right the high white wall, with crenulations painted in red, forms part of the rear wall of a Muslim Secondary School and a public library occupies rooms above the gateway. There are books in Urdu, Persian, and Arabic. The other wall exteriors have shops and dwellings climbing up them and immense activity going on within them; yet the courtyard maintains an air of utter tranquillity.

At one time this mosque used to stand in the centre of a spacious courtyard surrounded by a much lower perimeter wall.

The inside of the mosque itself has seen changes too. Most of the marble you see around you on the lower parts of the walls

Walk
6
৫৩৵৩

The Fatehpuri Masjid's Northern Entrance in the 1980s

has been added over the last twenty years. The clock over the Chandni Chowk gateway was put there in the 1970s.

The chief prayer leader in the mosque is called the Shahi Imam. The graves you see in the courtyard near the central pool are those of Shahi Imams who have served the Fatehpuri Mosque. The position is carried on by the Shahi Imam's eldest son. The present incumbent is proud of his direct relationship with the First, appointed by Shah Jahan, who served in the mosque when it was new. The round building surrounded by pierced screens used to house an old well.

At one time this religious building completely ceased to function as a mosque. As a consequence of the Uprising (1857) the British authorities closed it. Then in 1860, Muslims were once again allowed to use the mosque for worship but only the prayer hall and its platform. The courtyard was sold by auction and was bought by a Hindu banker, Lala Chunna Mal.

As Percival Spear says in his book *Twilight of the Mughals*, 'This was rather as though the choir and sanctuary of Westminster Abbey were released for Christian worship, the nave and transepts being sold for office space'.

It remained the family's private property until 1877 when the British authorities needed it back again to return to the Muslims. So the two parties came to an agreement. The Fatehpuri Mosque would be exchanged for four Indian villages worth 1,16,613 rupees. Lala Chunna Mal's family made a 300 per cent profit; in 1860 it had cost 40,000 rupees. The building was then fully reopened and became an important centre of intellectual life. Great religious debates were held here. Those between Bishop Lefroy on behalf of Christianity and Sharf-ul-Haq speaking for Islam attracted thousands of people.

Remember the name Chunna Mal. You'll be seeing where he and his family used to live once you're back in Chandni Chowk. Leave the mosque by the central gateway under the clock which takes you out facing Chandni Chowk. Put on your shoes.

Walk
6
୫᠗୦୫

The Walk to Haider Quli Khan's Gateway

On leaving the mosque, cross a very busy road (Katra Baryan) entering Chandni Chowk from the right, and with your back to the mosque walk down the right-hand side of Chandni Chowk.

You won't have gone more than 300 metres before you see a large metal veranda shading the pavement ahead. It is easily recognizable as there are ornate wrought iron flowers and leaves above the girders. Turn right before you walk under this veranda. (You turn right after Shop No. 326.) You'll walk down an entrance which goes under a wide vaulted gateway. Look carefully at the ceiling which at present is painted pale blue. Fortunately, flakes of paint have come off and you can see patches of the original colour of the stone—dark red—underneath. It looks unimpressive nowadays but in the past it was the entrance to splendour.

Haider Quli Khan

The gateway was built in the eighteenth century by a man whose name was Haider Quli and whose title was Khan. It led to a huge and beautiful mansion set within a lovely garden. Today it's all gone. What is interesting here is that this gateway marks the original street line. You can see how much wider the street used to be in the eighteenth century when, of course, there weren't hundreds of rickshaws, cars and motorbikes, just a few noblemen's elephants, horses and the measured tread of merchants' camel trains.

Haider Quli Khan was an unpleasant character. He was a senior Mughal official who had great power, first in the Deccan and then in Gujarat. He lined his own pockets while maintaining a flow of money to his imperial master. Haider Quli was even party to the murder of a nobleman who had earlier in his own career helped him considerably.

In the seventeenth and eighteenth centuries, there were several mansions like Haider Quli Khan's with entrance gateways along Chandni Chowk. In those days the street didn't have its present character based solely on intensive trading. As well as shops there used to be large gardens, inns and coffee shops, mansions, and most important of all, the freshness of the water channel, shaded by trees, running down the middle of the street. Return to Chandni Chowk and with your back to the gateway turn right and continue to walk along.

Finding Chunna Mal's Haveli

Continue walking along until you reach sets of traffic lights theoretically controlling the entrance and exit of vehicles into Chandni Chowk from a well-known, busy Old Delhi street on the right. This street is Ballimaran; if you need shoes or sandals you'll find a vast choice here as it is the centre of the leather trade. Cross over Ballimaran and walk on for about 50 metres; then stop, still on the right-hand side of Chandni Chowk, in front of Shop No. 4793 New National Store—it sells men's clothing. Look at the building across the street. Although it is extremely run down these days and there have been some hodgepodge additions to the top storey, it still retains some horizontal unity of design; you can see a distinctively long row of metal pillars fronting the first floor veranda and another higher row of metal railings on the storey above. Some of Lala Chunna Mal's twenty-first century descendants still occupy part of the haveli; the ground floor is completely commercial.

Lala Chunna Mal's Haveli

This is where Lala Chunna Mal, the man who bought the courtyard of the Fatehpuri Mosque, used to live. It was his haveli, his mansion. He was a highly respected merchant, his title Lala meaning just this—and it was indicative of the fact that while he had been wealthy before 1857, he managed to prosper even more so as a result of the Uprising of 1857. He was a merchant, banker and money lender who stayed loyal to the British (so it is claimed) when it was very dangerous to do so. The British had been forced out of the city in May 1857 and anyone sympathetic to their cause was in danger of losing their life. When the British retook Delhi in September they didn't want to re-establish the old Muslim aristocracy, so helped wealthy Hindu traders to become the new elite; a lalocracy.

Lala Chunna Mal

Once back in power, the British set about confiscating property belonging to the old Muslim nobility and allowed people like Chunna Mal to buy land and houses very cheaply. This house—his home—was magnificent; full of chandeliers and rich carpets. It was particularly beautiful at Hindu festival times such as Diwali.

Walk 6

A famous nineteenth century Muslim poet, Mirza Ghalib, commented bitterly on the contrasts he saw around him after the Uprising of 1857. 'While most of Delhi was plunged in grief and darkness,' he wrote, 'Chunna Mal's haveli was so flooded with light that it made night look like day.'

Your walk ends here.

Take a cycle or auto rickshaw back to your car at the Delhi Gate of the Red Fort car park or cross the road and walk to Chandni Chowk Metro Station. There are taxis at Delhi Main Railway Station.

Spices Reference Section

Familiar Items (In English and Hindi)

Nuts: almonds (badam), cashewnuts (kajoo), coconuts (nariyal), whole nutmegs (jaifer), peanuts (moong phali), pistachio nut (pista), walnuts (akhroi), betel nut for use in paan (supari).

Dried Fruits: raisins (kishmish), sultanas (munakka), dried dates (chhohara), dried figs (anjeer).

Ground Spices: They are some of the most common spices you see, piled up into pyramids. These are the following:

Red: Smooth chilli powder (bookanee lal mirch), finely chopped chillies (mota lal mirch).

Yellow: Ground turmeric (haldi powder).

Khaki: Ground coriander (dhania powder).

Off-White: Ground dried mango (aamchur).

Beige: Ground ginger.

Brown: A mixture for adding to fruit salad (fruit chaat mixture).

Spices in Sacks, Bins and Bottles

Aniseed (sauf), cardamom (elaichi), caraway (shahjeera), cinnamon sticks (dalchini), cummin seed (jeera), dried ginger (saunth), saffron (kesar), salt (namak), black salt (kala namak), black pepper (kali mirch), tamarind (imli), pomegranate seeds (anardana).

Less Familiar Produce

Reetha Nuts: These nuts are small, brown and shiny, and are put to surprising uses. You don't eat them but crack them, discard the hard black seeds, soak the brown outer skins overnight in hot water and then use them as a shampoo, or to clean silver, or wash silk and woollens. They're often called soap nuts.

For their use as shampoo, reetha nuts are often soaked with two other products you can buy here; a black seed-pod called shikakai and dried amla. Dried amla fruit is small, curly and black and from a distance an open sack of it looks as though it contains coking coal.

Burri Elaichi: This is a brown pod which often gives foreigners a fright when they first meet it in a curry or pulao. It's not the taste that frightens but the appearance. When cooked it can look very like a legless beetle.

Thandai: This is the name of the mixture you see containing rose petals. Together with almonds, bought separately and ground at home, it helps to make a refreshing cold drink. The mixture contains a variety of 'cooling' seeds such as melon, cucumber, poppy and sunflower as well as aniseed and pepper corns.

Phool Makhana: It looks very like smooth popcorn but is a variety of the lotus seed. It's white with brown speckles and very light. One way of preparing phool makhana is to deep-fry it in melted butter and salt and serve hot.

Heeng: It is a foul-smelling gum resin with medicinal properties. When heeng is fresh and soft it has the most pungent smell imaginable. (In Britain its name is asafoetida or fetid gum). It's worth buying a lump just to experience the power of the smell. Heeng is used as a condiment and to aid digestion, especially after large, vegetarian meals. It makes you burp. Babies are given minute amounts of heeng, with ground nutmeg and black salt, mixed together in a teaspoon with a little of their mother's milk, to relieve wind. In relation to the cost of other spices, heeng is expensive.

Walk
6
ৰ্তৰ্তৰ্ত

Walk 7:
Sadhus and Trains

Lost palatial grandeur, Hindu holy men (sadhus), trains and Delhi's Town Hall. A walk into the past which makes a good early morning weekday walk. You could do the walk on Sunday if you are slim! This is because a set of gates to Begum Samru's old palace will probably be chained together, as the shops behind it are closed, but averagely thin people can squeeze through. Some of the electrical shops in the Lajpat Rai market will be closed on a Sunday too: the holy men, the trains, the park and the Town Hall are always there.

This is an interestingly varied walk which takes over two and a half hours to complete. However, if you want to cut the walk short you could finish after seeing the sadhus at Bankhandi. Ending your walk here leaves you very near to the main road, Shyama Prasad Mukherji Marg, where there are cycle and auto rickshaws, or you could pick up a taxi from Delhi Main Railway Station.

Places of Interest
LAJPAT RAI ELECTRICAL GOODS MARKET
ARYA SAMAJ BUILDING
BHAGIRATH PALACE AND BEGUM SAMRU
OLD DELHI RAILWAY STATION (DELHI MAIN)
THE SADHUS OF BANKHANDI
MAHATMA GANDHI PARK
OLD DELHI TOWN HALL

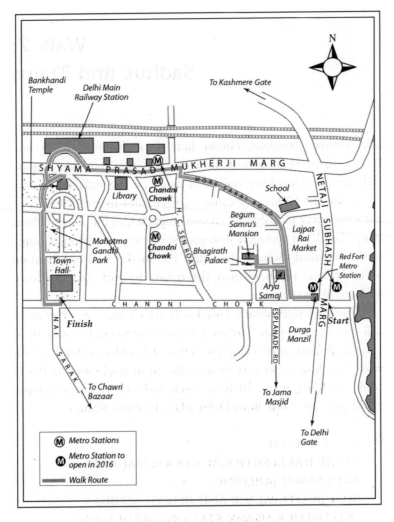

Walk 7: Route Map

Getting There

By Car

Park in the well-known and well-organized Red Fort car park in front of the fort's Delhi Gate. It's approached from Nishad Raj Marg. Charges vary according to length of stay but are always reasonable. Then, with your back to the Red Fort, take an auto or cycle rickshaw to the right-hand side of Chandni Chowk.

By Metro

Take the Yellow Line to Chandni Chowk station. Exit at Gate 5. Follow the main flow of people into the sunshine and you'll pass a large Hindu temple to Lord Shani on your right which is famous for its team of seven white horses above the entrance. On your left you'll pass a motorbike park. When this path reaches H.C. Sen Road, turn right and you'll see the blue and white dry fountain of Bhai Mati Das Chowk. Cross the road and continue walking towards the Red Fort until Chandni Chowk ends. Stop under a large tree on your left which has its trunk surrounded by the red wooden walls of a temple enclosing numerous shrines.

Walk
7
ཚོགས

The Walk

Now turn round and with your back to the Red Fort, look more carefully at the little Hindu temple built around the large tree. There are coloured squares of glass on the sides and the temple is festooned with bells and garlands. It's the Durga Manzil, which was built in 1948. It is a strange place as three sides contain Hindu shrines and has a priest who seems to live above in a kind of tree house, but one side is a popular spicy fruit salad (fruit chaat) shop; the dishes are pushed through a window in a wooden wall. It seems such a bizarre juxtaposition! Selling the chaat raises money for the temple.

Climb the steps immediately behind the temple as they lead to the electrical shops of the Lajpat Rai Market. Notice the trees on either side of the steps.

Lajpat Rai Market

The trees are Pipal trees (*Ficus religiosa*) and are all that's left of a park that used to be here before the market was built in the 1950s. It was called Pipal Park.

It had to go, as a new market was needed to house the many refugee traders who'd left their businesses in West Punjab (now in Pakistan) and come to Delhi after the partition of India in 1947. If you look at the shop names you'll see that many are owned by Punjabis. Now it's the centre of the electronic goods trade.

Many Delhi people must have regretted the disappearance of the park, not only because it added greenery to the city but also because it had strong political associations. Great nationalist leaders addressed meetings here, especially in 1919, when there was a good deal of political activity against British authority and the new laws framed by Mr Justice Rowlatt. (These laws provided for internment without trial for political activists and gave judges the right to try political cases without juries.) One such leader was Swami Shraddhanand and you'll be meeting him, as a statue, later.

Walk
7
ೞೕಞ

Walk along and stop when you come to a gap in the row of shops, above a flight of steps which overlook Chandni Chowk. It's opposite a shop named Super Sales India and is a great place for taking photographs of the traffic snarl-ups in the road below! As you walk on a little you'll come to a Hindu shrine on the left under a pipal tree. This tree is sacred to Lord Vishnu, the preserver and controller of harmony in the world. (P.P Jewellers support him too!) You will pass dozens of shrines under trees on this walk as you are in the northern part of Old Delhi, which is the predominantly Hindu part. South of the Jama Masjid is the predominantly Muslim area where you're never far from a mosque.

Continue walking straight ahead and you'll meet another road with a big 'AHUJA P-A System' sign facing you. Turn right and walk up the road. You are now in Dewan Hall Road. You'll pass

Lajpat Rai Market—the Entrance from Chandni Chowk in the 1980s

the entrance to the Moti (Pearl) cinema on your left. If you're interested in Bollywood wander in and consider the week's movie. Going to the cinema is quite an experience, even if you can't understand Hindi, so make a note of the times and prices and come back later. A few metres further on, you come to a large grey stone building with bright orange temple flags flying from its roof. This is the Arya Samaj building and is called the Dewan Hall.

The Arya Samaj (The Society of Nobles)

The Arya Samaj movement began in the 1880s. It is an egalitarian reform sect of Hinduism which emphasizes not simply the need to uphold the Hindu faith but to serve one's fellow men through practical good work. The Arya Samaj runs schools, especially girls' schools, colleges, and helps the poor. In the past, members of this sect provided money most generously to feed famine victims who flocked into Delhi in the 1890s.

Walk
7
ॐ

Its members worship one God and have an intense dislike of idolatry. Their form of worship is very simple: passages from the Vedas (Hindu holy books) are recited and hymns sung whilst clarified butter is burnt over a fire.

The movement puts great stress on India's past and patriotism. This is why it was so in tune with the nationalist movement of the early 1900s. Swami Shraddhanand was a member of the Arya Samaj. There's a huge meeting hall on the ground floor of the building and above are rooms used by Arya Samaj members temporarily visiting Delhi, but the length of stay is restricted to between three and five days. The temple is open between 6.00 a.m. and 10.00 p.m., but only to members.

At the corner of the Arya Samaj building turn left. This road is called Bhagirath Palace, Dewan Hall.

Bhagirath Palace and Begum Samru's Old Home

Walk up Bhagirath Place, Dewan Hall Road, towards some trees in the distance. You'll pass several little food stalls on the right

selling samosas, fried sandwiches and gulab jamuns. The stalls on
the left sell garlands, paper lanterns, tinsel decorations and fairy
lights. These trees surround a small Hindu temple—only, you can
no longer see it for electrical stalls selling fairy lights. This must
be fairy light wholesale world! Look out for Shop No. 1520
Bhagirath Place on the right (J.J. Trading Co. Domestic Electrical
Appliances), and a little ahead on your right you'll see a pair of
open black metal gates, with spikes on the top. They are open
from 9.30 a.m. to 10 p.m. every day except Sundays. Turn right
here and walk past a few medical related shops, then turn left and
look up. You'll see the pediment of a large building with 'Lloyd's
Bank Limited' still visible. Lloyd's Bank moved out long ago but
this is the building you want to find. Walk round to a flight of
steps leading up to a colonnaded veranda, and amongst the tea
stalls, squatting porters and urban sprawl, read about the house
in its glory days and its famous builder, Begum Samru. (There's
a stone slab describing Begum Samru in English and Hindi but
it has become difficult to read.)

Walk
7
ॐ

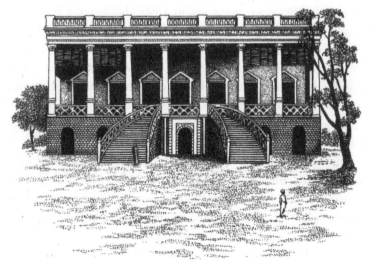

Begum Samru's Mansion in the 1840s

The building was owned by a very intelligent Kashmiri Muslim woman who had the wit to run a large estate and maintain a reliable and disciplined private army that the Mughal emperor of the time (Shah Alam) could call upon for help. He did so many times and it was his gratitude that maintained her wealth and status. She'd married a wealthy man in her youth called Walther Reinhardt, having met him when she was a dancing girl. He was a soldier of fortune, originally from Luxembourg, who had indeed made a fortune in India, yet rarely looked pleased with life. His friends called him 'sombre' and this became Samru. Begum Samru became a Christian after her husband's death. It wasn't because she wished to be united with him in heaven but because she employed European Christian officers in her army and they had persuaded her to convert to Christianity. Begum Samru's Christian name was Joanna, given to her by a Roman Catholic priest in 1781, in Agra. Brought up a Muslim she maintained Muslim habits of dress, always covering her head, even though she built a Roman Catholic cathedral in Sardanha.

She held magnificent balls and entertainments in this house in the early 1800s. At one party in 1809, the dancing girls were so weighed down with thick gold rings and bells around their legs that one guest felt them to be shackled and unable to leap even if they'd wished to. Imagine the view from the balcony in the early nineteenth century! It was of a lovely garden stretching to Chandni Chowk itself. Now the Bank of India occupies much of the space behind the old facade. The debris of the ages seems to have engulfed it!

One sad episode in the building's past concerns the old king, Bahadur Shah, the last Mughal ruler. He'd been involved in the Uprising of 1857 and was brought here after his capture in September of that year. The king was 'most wretched and disliked intensely being stared at by Europeans'—so claims Percival Spear in his book *Twilight of the Mughals*. He was quite obviously wretched, having lost his throne and with two of his sons dead and on public display in Chandni Chowk.

The building was originally referred to as Begum Samru's Palace, but after changing hands a few times it was bought, in 1940, by a merchant, Lala Bhagirath Mai. His name is now synonymous with this area, and the area itself with wholesale chemists and medical supplies. Walk back the way you came to the black gate. You'll pass shops selling 'cervial collors' and 'alu' (aluminium) crutches and medical X-ray film. After this point turn left and retrace your steps back to the road you left at the Arya Samaj building. It was Dewan Hall Road. Refer to your sketch map on page 106. Continue walking along this busy road away from Chandni Chowk. There's another Hindu shrine on your right, and when you come to a junction, turn left.

You are now in the tree-lined and well-shaded More Sarai Road. You'll walk about 500 metres along this road, and as you leave the dozens of tiny shops selling new electrical goods, you come to the second-hand section where you see ancient TV's , earphones, old cables or parts of radios and odd bits of plugs. Now and again, you pass shops filled to the brim with used cardboard boxes, and towards the end you see men and women (scavengers) sorting glass bottles and plastics into various piles, although there are far fewer of them in this road than in the past. This street has gone up in the world!

Walk
7
ॐ✿ॐ

Walking to Old Delhi Railway Station (Delhi Main)

When the quiet road you're on suddenly ends at a junction with a main road, the traffic ahead is a shock. Any time after 10 a.m., the road is packed with cars, motorbikes, rickshaws, buses, bullock carts, bicycles and people. This is because you are near two very busy roads, H.C. Sen Road and Shyama Prasad Mukherji Marg. The one facing you is H.C. Sen Marg; the one to your right which passes Delhi Main Railway Station is Shyama Prasad Mukherji Marg. Dodge the traffic and cross H.C. Sen Marg. Don't put any faith at all in the zebra crossing. You'll see Old Delhi Railway

Station looming large, red and turreted on your right. Nowadays the road is just another busy, run-of-the-mill Delhi highway; in the 1870s it was called Queen's Road (to honour Queen Victoria, naturally) and was one of the most beautiful roads in Delhi. It was bordered by gardens and fine public buildings.

Stay on the left-hand side of the road until you've passed Delhi Public Library, then find an opportunity to cross Shyama Prasad Mukherji Marg and enter the station area. Enter as soon as you can and begin to explore the area. You'll see booking offices, sleeping dogs, illuminated noticeboards listing trains with wonderful sounding names and dozens of families resting on blankets in every shady spot. Walk towards the station's main entrance foyer. It's easy to find as it is in the middle of the complex in the red turreted section. There's a clock tower above the central arch and a large grey 'Delhi' written in Hindi and English against a red background. You'll be asked to pass through a relaxed security check; subject yourself to a body swipe and a bag X-ray (although others seem to find ways round), and enter the station concourse.

Walk
7

Old Delhi Railway Station

It's a shady place and there are many people lying about in family groups, resting until their trains are due. If you enjoy stations there's a lot to interest you. The station is very much calmer than it used to be and the platform signs much clearer. Sadly, the refreshingly honest noticeboard, 'Trains Running Late', has gone. However, there is still an 'Emergency Notice Board' which notes 'Special Trains for Festival Rush' and then lists the extra ones put on to Patna, Varanasi, Gaya and Chandigarh in order to get temporary residents such as migrant workers back to their homes for Diwali. And McDonalds has arrived! Fancy a spicy cheese burger? There's one on Platform 4.

One experience which is well worth having before leaving the station, is to climb up the steps to the walkway, here called the

'Foot Over Bridge' which crosses over all the lines. Walk its full length to Platform 16. If a train has just arrived at Platform 16 it can be a squash, but it's worth it. You can see if anyone is risking a quick illegal dash across the tracks. Fewer do these days. It's also a good vantage point for taking photographs. When you've had enough of platforms and trains retrace your steps and leave the station and return to the main road. Seeing 'Delux Toilet' on a building on your right as you walk back might tempt you to nip inside. If you are desperate it's a very useful facility, however far from luxurious in the 'Imperial Hotel' sense of the word. 'Basic' would be better, although the women's toilets do have a handy 6-inch nails sticking out of toilet walls for bags. Charges: 5 rupees for the cloakroom (women), 2 rupees for the men's toilets, 1 rupee for a urinal. Very fair!

Walking to Bankhandi

To reach your next stop cross the main road (Shyama Prasad Mukherji Marg). Look for a set of traffic lights, because when they turn red you can actually cross. Once on the opposite side of the road turn right; you'll see a large blue sign across the road pointing left to the Town Hall. You won't go this far but aim in that direction. Take the first road on your left and after a few metres you'll be opposite the ornate entrance to this strange, loose arrangement of shrines and living space for holy men that is known as Bankhandi. Brass statues of Durga's lions and Shiva's bull, garlanded and polished, keep guard. If you wish to descend the steps and walk around the shrines take off your shoes and leave them in the small shoe room on the right next to the entrance. You can leave your motorbike helmet there too! If you are content to view the area from above, stay shod.

Bankhandi and its Sadhus

Although locally known as Bankhandi, the full name is Prachin Shri Bankhandi Mahadev Mandir. The word 'bankhandi' is made up of a word for jungle (ban) and another for small area (khandi), but when this area was really wild must have been a very long time ago. It's claimed that all the main Gods in the Hindu pantheon can be worshipped at this one site. The main shrine is called the Holy Baba Temple and is easily distinguishable even though small, as it is in the middle of the courtyard, at present covered by a yellow tarpaulin and surrounded by a delicate red bamboo railing. Depending on the time of day this area can be very crowded or completely deserted. The number of sadhus living here varies as they only stay whilst passing through Delhi. Sadhus are ascetics who have decided to renounce life's creature comforts and live a harsh, simple existence. They are trying to obtain moksha—liberation from the constant cycle of rebirth, through concentrating on prayer and meditation. Sometimes, there are many wandering around; at other times you see very few. Usually there are between twenty and thirty sadhus living here and they stay until they feel the call of God to move somewhere else—such as Rishikesh or Haridwar in the Himalayas. Some live in small shacks behind the shrines and others under loose arrangements of canvas. If you stand facing the main shrine, this 'sadhu living area' is over to your right. You catch glimpses of orange and red-robed turbaned men squatting or lying on platforms or cooking over small fires. When writing this guide book the head sadhu was Guruji Bharatpuriji and he lives here permanently giving advice to those who seek it and blessings. He is much revered by the rank and file sadhus!

The area is particularly busy during the monsoon season as the resident sadhus are joined by orange-clad men (followers of Shiva but not full-time holy men), on pilgrimages. These people are called kavariya. They walk, carrying a colourful, tinsel decorated bamboo yoke across one shoulder from the ends of which dangle pots in baskets. They are walking from their local temples to Haridwar to collect water from the river Ganges. They then return to their own Shiva temples with this sacred water.

Sometimes, this involves much suffering as their feet become blistered and walking is obviously painful. Yet they walk on as they have made promises to do so, either in gratitude to Shiva for a favour granted or in the hope of a favour being given. Leave the shrines, climb the steps and collect your shoes.

The temple entrance is at the apex of the curve of a road. With your back to this entrance, turn left and walk along the pavement of the left-hand curve. There are many openings in the walls so you can easily look down onto the shrines and living area. A particularly good gap is one at which there is a horizontal line of bells. Many people who haven't time to visit the shrines themselves pray from the pavement here. Keep walking left for about ten more paces and stop at a large flat concrete block surrounded by trees and covered in birdseed and sweet corn. You'll see pigeons and crows, tiny squirrels and rats feeding together happily, all on top of the block. The sadhus put out food and there's plenty to go round. The rats live at the base of the block and you see them peeping out of their holes and running around most confidently. St Francis of Assisi would approve! Pity about the rubbish.

Walk
7
ॐ☯ॐ

Mahatma Gandhi Park

Walk just a few metres further along and look left through the railings and the palm trees into the middle of the park and try to see a statue of Gandhi. He's depicted in a typical pose, staff in hand as though leading the Salt March, and stands aloft a pink plinth. You have to do this before you reach the first gate on your left as the trees mask the statue completely here. The gate will most probably be locked as it is only open for a few hours in the morning (5 a.m. to 8 a.m.) and a few in the evening (5 p.m. to 8.30 p.m.) and on Sundays. To most people, Mahatma Gandhi needs no introduction as he is undoubtedly the most famous Indian politician of the Quit India movement. His policy of peaceful non-cooperation with the British was most effective and they quit in 1947. There are many museums dedicated to him in Delhi and the house in which he was assassinated is open to the public.

This park, behind the Town Hall, wasn't always Mahatma Gandhi Park. It used to be called Queen's Park but was commonly known as Company Bagh (Company Garden)—a triumph for trade (the British East India Company) over Queen Victoria. But whatever the name, it has been a popular open air space for a very long time. In the 1880s, it acted as an outdoor club for Delhi's intelligentsia, doctors and lawyers, judges, teachers, and administrators who worked in Chandni Chowk. It had lots of shady trees, an open air space for cricket, and a military band played here once a week. Cricket is still played here on a Sunday by lots of enthusiastic boys in teams dotted all over the park, who are delighted to have some space to hit one for six for a change.

Continue walking straight ahead for about 400 metres until you reach Chandni Chowk. Turn left and after a few metres look at the large yellow and white building on your left. It's Old Delhi Town Hall.

Walk
7
ॐ

Old Delhi Town Hall

This very 'British' building was begun in 1860 and finished in 1865 and didn't start life as a town hall at all. At first, it was called the Lawrence Institute and was an educational and cultural centre, but in 1866 the Municipality bought it and squeezed out the centre of higher studies, Delhi College, which it had housed. (If you do many of the walks you'll realize that over its long life Delhi College has been housed in several different places.)

Most of the rooms became offices, carrying out the tasks of town halls the world over; digging drains, making roads, setting up schools and collecting taxes. However, rooms were set aside for a library and the European Club. Public meetings were held here too. In 1892, 2,000 people gathered here to discuss the new plague regulations. Walk round to its ornate front facade.

Look at the statue. There used to be a bronze statue of Queen Victoria here but she's been moved and in her place is Swami Shraddhanand, the Arya Samaj nationalist leader you read about earlier. Queen Victoria is said to have found lodgings in Delhi College of Art.

Swami Shraddhanand

Like Mahatma Gandhi, he had a legal background and was a superb orator. In 1919, he spoke very movingly at the funerals of men killed by the police when breaking up nationalist meetings. And like Gandhi, he was assassinated. He was killed by a fanatic who'd asked for and been given hospitality in his home.

Nowadays he's usually got pigeons on his shoulders. Hundreds of these birds perch on the cornices of the building as they are fed so often. You gain spiritual merit from feeding the birds, and seed and grain are on sale outside. A large plate of seed costs about ten or fifteen rupees and the smaller ones less.

Next to the birdseed sellers there are always rows of daily wage carpenters, plasterers and painters resting on their haunches, tools of their respective trades close at hand, patiently waiting to be hired.

It's hard to believe as you gaze at today's congestion in Chandni Chowk, that in the middle of the road, just here, the British built a neo-Gothic clock tower, somewhat resembling London's Big Ben. Some Delhi folk liked it, others hated it, but it never worked properly as the weight of pigeons sitting on the hands disturbed the mechanism. To build the clock tower in 1868, the British filled in the pool that Shah Jahan's daughter had designed and which had reflected the silvery moonlight so beautifully giving Chandni Chowk (Moonlit Square) its name. The clock tower collapsed in 1952.

Your walk ends here.

Take a cycle or auto rickshaw back to your car at the Red Fort's Delhi Gate. You can see the Red Fort's domes in the

Walk
7

distance as you look down Chandni Chowk.

If you arrived by Metro you're quite near Chandni Chowk Metro Station. Continue walking towards the Red Fort then turn left at the first road you come to (Town Hall Marg)—you'll have one side of the Town Hall on your left. Then, after about 200 metres, cross over the road and turn right at the first turning on the right. You'll walk in front of a Ramjas Senior Secondary School No. 3 Gate. There's a little park on the opposite corner of the road you want. This road will lead you into Chandni Chowk Metro Station.

There are also taxis to be had in front of Delhi Main Railway Station.

Walk
7
ॐॐॐ

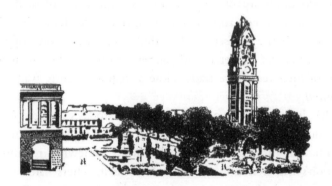

Nineteenth-century View of the Clock Tower and Delhi Town Hall

Walk 8:
Spiritual Chandni Chowk

Garlands, a temple, a gurdwara, a mosque and gory paintings. This is a good short early morning walk. It's advisable to enter the Gauri Shankar temple before 10 a.m. as it closes at 11 a.m. It reopens at 4 p.m. and stays open until 11 p.m. This temple opens its doors very early in the morning at 4.30 a.m. The Sikh gurdwara is open all day. The mosque is too, except for the usual proviso that it is closed to non-Muslims at prayer times. Don't worry about the mosque being closed because it's only the site's historical significance that is important in this walk.

Places of Interest
THE GARLAND SELLERS OF CHANDNI CHOWK
THE GAURI SHANKAR HINDU TEMPLE
THE SIKH SISGANJ GURDWARA
THE SUNHERI MOSQUE
THE DRY FOUNTAIN IN BHAI MATI DAS CHOWK
THE BHAI MATI DAS MUSEUM

Getting There

By Car
Park in the large, well-organized and well-known Red Fort car park in front of the fort's Delhi Gate. It's approached from Nishad Raj Marg. Charges vary according to length of stay but are always

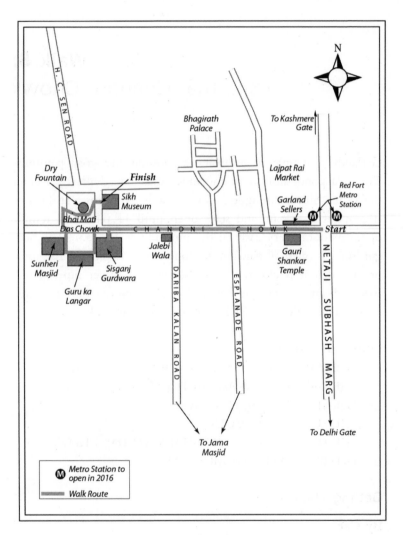

Walk 8: Route Map

reasonable. It's open from 8 a.m. to 10 p.m. Then take a cycle or scooter rickshaw to the start of your walk which is opposite the Jain temple on Chandhi Chowk. With your back to the Red Fort, this is on the right-hand side of the road.

By Metro

Take the Yellow Line to Chandni Chowk station. Exit by Gate 5. The station is a little misleadingly named as it is not on Chandni Chowk itself but about a ten-minute walk away. If you follow the main flow of people exiting Gate 5, you'll pass a large Hindu temple to Lord Shani on your right which is famous for its magnificent team of life-size sculpted horses above the entrance. On your left you'll pass a huge motorbike park. When this path reaches H.C. Sen Road, turn right and you'll see the blue and white fountain of Bhai Mati Das Chowk straight ahead. Walk left to the garland sellers.

The Walk

Walk
8
ঙ৩৺৩ঔ

The Garland Sellers

Walk away from the Red Fort along the right side of Chandni Chowk. You often have to walk behind a row of movable, yellow Delhi Police barriers. You'll soon come to a row of eight small garland sellers' shops. The shop keepers say they've been making and selling garlands here for over a hundred years. The smell from the flowers is lovely and such a pleasant change! If you look closely you'll see men using special 10-inch long needles to thread jasmine, white tuber roses, small chrysanthemums, roses and orchids into intricate patterns to make the most impressive of wedding garlands. Take one off its hook—it's surprisingly heavy! There are piles of simpler marigold garlands on the counters too and sometimes, hanging delicately across several hooks, are nets made of flowers to decorate wedding cars. You can buy one garland or order dozens for a family event, as these men—as everywhere else in Old Delhi—are wholesalers.

The temple you will be visiting is on the left side of Chandni Chowk, but to get a better view of it stop in front of one of the first garland sellers—Shop No. 7, Shri Gauri Shankar Flower Shop—and look at the white stone temple building across the road. You'll see a mass of orange pennants fluttering in the sunshine and Hindi script on the facade. This building is the Gauri Shankar Hindu temple.

Gauri Shankar Temple

Gauri Shankar is another way of saying Parvati-Shiva, i.e. Parvati, the wife of Lord Shiva. This is one of Delhi's most important Shiva temples, as one of the symbols of Lord Shiva kept inside is 800 years old.

Lord Shiva is one of the three great Lords of Hinduism: Brahma (creation), Vishnu (preservation) and Shiva (destruction and recreation). Each of these Lords expresses a different aspect of the one Supreme or Absolute Being who is the ultimate goal of all Hindu worship. Inside the temple there are many idols but these are mere 'props for the neophyte', says Swami Sivananda. As your intellectual discipline increases you need them less and less. At the same time, there is never any discredit attached to relying on idols to concentrate your prayers, as they are always felt to be effective channels of devotion.

Look at the Hindi at the base of the spire. Translated, it means 'Shivalaya Apa Ganga Dhar'. Shivalaya means a house for Lord Shiva. Apa Ganga Dhar is a man's name. He was a Hindu soldier, a Maratha who had always worshipped Lord Shiva. But when, during a battle, he was confronted with such overwhelming odds that he thought he would surely die without divine help, he promised to build a temple for Lord Shiva were he to survive. The soldier survived and kept his promise. You can see the size of a smaller, older temple once you're inside, but it has been built over and around so much that the newer structures dwarf and hide the old. The second inscription in Hindi, just above the three central

Shiva and Parvati

windows, is witness to one of these more recent additions. It tells you that it was built in 1959 by Seth Beni Pershad Jaipuria.

Cross over the road; you can always find a gap in the road dividers somewhere. There are two entrances, but the one you will use is near to Umrao Singh Primary School (established in 1939). There are cartoon characters stuck on the walls. The entrance you want has carved chains and bells down the flanking marble pillars. If you are not familiar with Hindu practices, take a look before entering at the goods on sale a little to the left of the entrance. These men are selling everything a devout Hindu needs to offer to Shiva. There are baskets of rose petals, marigolds, bilva leaves and cotton thread candles in tiny clay bowls The sweet shops nearby have ready made up bags of sweets, with just a few inside, to give as offerings too. Prepare to enter the temple.

Before you enter through the flight of marble steps, leave your shoes with the man in the corridor on the left. He'll put them away in a shoe rack and give you a number. The service is free but he does have a dish into which you can place a little money for the service on your return. If you wish to keep wearing your socks it is allowed, only, be warned upstairs is often sluiced so they'll end up wet. Retrace your steps back down the 'shoe alley', go outside for a step or two, then walk up the narrow marble entrance staircase.

Climb the steps and enter the temple. You'll emerge on its left-hand side. Don't think that by entering you will upset a Hindu priest or be intrusive to the worshippers. As long as your clothing is modest, you don't stand in the way of people wishing to pray to Shiva and your behaviour is respectful and interested, the priests will make you welcome. There's a friendly atmosphere. Hinduism isn't evangelical so no one will try to convert you to the faith but they will try to help you to understand the behaviour you see. Most devotees will ignore you completely to concentrate on their prayers. The occasional holy man may ask you for alms. Some among the old ladies, probably widows, might too.

Inside the Temple

The Courtyard

At the top of the steps, turn right and walk into the courtyard. It's a pleasant place in which there's always something happening. The busiest part is often on the left where there's a row of taps and nearby a table full of steel bowls. This is where devotees get the pot and the water they need to use as a libation for the lingam. Near the taps, just a little further in towards the temple, you'll see two rough blocks of red stone which are used for making sandalwood paste. There's always a piece of sandalwood on a block; a devotee adds a little water, rubs the wood against the stone for a few minutes, then carefully collects the paste in the palm of one hand. This will be used for anointing Shiva and then afterwards the devotee will put some on his own forehead. Across the courtyard, there's a metal container for offerings of cotton thread candles in front of Shiva's large brass trident. At any time of the day you will see worshippers ringing bells to alert the Gods to their prayers, moving between and around the shrines, singing holy songs, talking together in little groups, or sometimes just sitting very still in meditation.

The Shrines

If you are unfamiliar with Hindu temples and devotional behaviour, find a quiet corner of the shady carpeted hall behind the marble flagged courtyard and take a few minutes to read about the main shrine.

The Main Shrine to Shiva and Parvati (Gauri Shankar)

This shrine is in a central position behind the three sets of wooden doors. If the doors facing you are closed, enter from a side door. Inside this shrine is the temple's most revered symbol of Shiva, the 800-year-old lingam. The lingam is a brown, phallus-shaped stone on which is a geological 'picture' of another phallus. The brown stone lingam is encased in a marble representation of the female organ which itself is encased in a beautiful silver surround, ornamented with snakes. It's often hard to see the lingam itself as although quite wide it isn't very tall and is usually covered in marigold garlands and bilva leaves. You have to bend down in front of the main shrine to see it.

Devotees pour libations of water or milk over the lingam and place bilva leaves and other offerings on and around it. To a Hindu, a lingam is much more than a simple fertility symbol as it represents a cosmic pillar, the centre of the universe, life itself. The water falls into a marble trough in which there are carvings of all the members of Lord Shiva's family. There's Lord Shiva himself and his bull Nandi, his wife Parvati and his two sons Kartik—the

God of war, and Ganesh—the elephant-headed God.

Above the lingam is a silver water vessel; behind it, a silver canopy containing the silver-crowned idols of Lord Shiva and Parvati, both bedecked with jewellery; behind them is a superb silver-plated wall depicting episodes from the life of Lord Shiva. A priest (pujari) sits in the shrine on the left and receives offerings. All food offerings are later given away to the poor. On the wall to the right is a startling neon sign, in red and blue. A mantra commonly chanted here is Lord Shiva's mantra, 'Om namah Shivaya'. The whole atmosphere in this shrine is one of intense dedication to Lord Shiva, whose power devotees feel to be so great and whose help they seek so reverentially. You feel this particularly strongly on a Monday which is the day of the week associated with Shiva, when the temple is very busy indeed. The temple manager claims that thousands of devotees worship here on a Monday. Devotees indicate their submission to Lord Shiva by either lowering their body posture in some way or prostrating themselves fully along the floor. If you see a person crossing his arms across his chest and pulling at his earlobes, it means he is admitting his faults, asking for forgiveness, and promising to mend his ways. A person beating the side of his head with his own clenched fists is asking Lord Shiva to help him learn. It's as though he's trying to force the knowledge into his head.

Walk
8
ॐॐॐ

As mentioned above, there's always a pujari in attendance at this shrine, one of the ten or so employed by this busy temple. A pujari is a man whose work involves helping devotees to carry out rituals correctly. They are distinguished by their white robes, necklaces of nuts, three lines of sandal paste smeared across their foreheads and almost shaven heads. (Not all the pujaris, however, bear all these signs of recognition.)

(If you'd like to read more about Hinduism turn to the Historical Appendix, 'Notes on Hinduism', at the end of this walk.)

Visit the shrines. The diagram below will help but please ask the pujaris for information. They can distinguish between all the Gods.

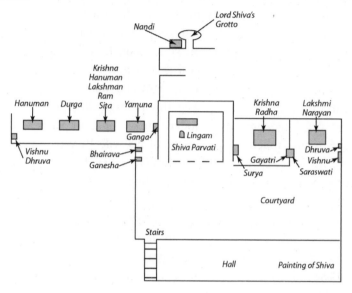

The Layout of the Shrines

The Marble Chair of Bhagwat Swaroop Brahmachari

With your back to the steps you came up by, cross the marble courtyard to the right-hand side, then walk forward and look left behind the large pierced screen. You'll see a marble chair. There's a garlanded picture on the chair and a pair of sandals rest on a cushion. Above it are photographs of a smiling old man. He's Bhagwat Swaroop Brahmachari, a Hindu saint who lived in this temple for fifty-four years. He entered it at the age of eleven. He lived a very simple life, eating fruit, flowers, leaves and nothing else. His whole life was spent worshipping Lord Shiva and giving advice to the many who sought it.

Now that he can no longer sit here in person and give advice, some of his teachings have been written down to help devotees follow the godly path to achieving enlightenment.

There's an amazing grotto to Lord Shiva at the back of the temple behind all the shrines, so don't leave without seeing it. To find it, cross the courtyard to the side you came in by and walk straight ahead. You'll find yourself in a passage with the main Gauri Shankar shrine on your right. It will lead you into a covered courtyard where food is distributed to holy men and poor Hindus, often women. Turn right and walk into the centre of this courtyard and then from this point, walk straight ahead. There is a huge, powerful, modern image of Lord Shiva within a cave, with a much smaller image of his wife Parvati suspended above his head. Nowadays, he is loosely covered in a loin cloth but formerly you could see him standing on a lion's skin simply swathed in snakes. There's a large brass bull on the left. This is Nandi, Shiva's transport. Retrace your steps to the exit.

Before you leave, or as you are leaving, you may be given a few sweets as 'blessed food' called prasad.

Please don't reject prasad, or accept it and then throw it away. This kind of behaviour might give offence. Prasad doesn't have to be eaten in the temple itself. So, if for religious reasons or because you don't like the sweets themselves you don't want to eat them, just keep them, and give them away to a child in Chandni Chowk.

Giving prasad to others is absolutely acceptable. Many devotees take prasad home to share with their family and friends.

Walking to the Sisganj Gurdwara and Preparing to Enter

Leave the temple and collect your shoes. Stay on the same side of Chandni Chowk and walk swiftly past the dozens of bags, watches, shoes and clothing shops; cross the wide expanse of Esplanade Road and then a little later, the narrow entrance to Dariba Kalan. You know you've crossed this one as the famous Jalebi Wala sweet snack seller is on the one corner and his sign flashes in neon glory. Keep walking until you've reached a marble paved area which indicates the approach of the gurdwara. There's shady basement area before you reach the main entrance, in the corner of which is the Sikh Information office. The function of the room is written on the window. If you would like someone to guide you around the gurdwara then please ask for help here. The service is free. You must leave any cigarettes, drugs or alcohol you may have with you in this room. If you are bareheaded you will be given a headscarf. If are bareheaded but don't want to spend time in the Information Room, a scarf will be handed to you as you climb the steps into the prayer hall of the gurdwara itself.

Leave the first basement area and walk a few paces further along until you come to the gurdwara's main entrance. It's a very crowded area with a lot of washing activity going on; you'll see buckets and taps. Immediately behind a portion of the marble pavement, which is constantly being sprinkled with water from a low pipe, there's a flight of steps which lead into the worship hall. Don't try to ascend these steps now as you need to take off your shoes (and socks) and leave them in the shoe room first. The shoe room is a surprisingly large, shady basement area which is on your left after the main entrance's flight of steps. It's always very busy! You walk down a few steps, sit on long padded benches, take off your shoes and hand them in at one of many kiosks lining the walls. You'll receive a metal token in exchange. Again, the service is free. To keep yourself in touch with this particular guided walk please don't leave the shoe room by the side exit. Leave the way you came in and return to Chandni Chowk. Walk a few paces to your right, cross the watery slab and climb the main flight of steps into the worship hall. There is a striking Sikh guard, clad in orange, who is handing out head scarves on the left. At the top of the stairs turn left, and walk around.

Walk
8

Guru Tegh Bahadur

There are ten Sikh Gurus. The one who is revered and remembered here is Guru Tegh Bahadur who was the ninth Guru and was martyred under a banyan tree in 1675. You'll see part of this banyan tree inside the worship hall. This Guru was put to death by the Mughal Emperor Aurangzeb because he stood up against the emperor's orders. Aurangzeb was persecuting brahmins who refused to renounce their Hindu faith and (to Aurangzeb) their idolatrous ways. Ironically, Guru Tegh Bahadur was also preaching against idolatry but he objected to Aurangzeb's use of force to achieve conversions. The persecuted brahmins had asked the Guru to help them and he gave his word that he would. After being forced to watch three close friends and followers cruelly murdered, he himself was beheaded. His head was taken to a town in the Punjab where it was cremated. His body was snatched by some of his followers and cremated secretly about two miles south of here. One of the followers set his whole house on fire to hide the smoke of the funeral pyre he'd prepared in its midst.

Walk
8
ੴ

Inside the Sisganj Gurdwara

Sis means head, Ganj settlement, therefore 'head settlement' because a Sikh martyr was beheaded here.

Visitors are made to feel extremely welcome because Sikhs believe that all the people attending a gurdwara make up a community in which God is the father and the people brothers and sisters. As you enter the worship hall someone may introduce themselves and offer to show you around.

The worship hall, with its glowing golden shrine and beautiful chandeliers, is truly magnificent. The focus of the room is the Sikh Holy Book, the Guru Granth Sahib which is covered by rich cloths and flower garlands and lies beneath a golden canopy. A priest is always in attendance. There are garlands of flowers piled up against the base of the golden canopy and many vases of gladioli lead up to it. At one side, a small group of musicians sing hymns from the Holy Book throughout the day. At night, the Holy Book is carried to a special area for safekeeping which contains a bed. As you walk around you'll see that one corner of

The Sisganj Gurdwara, Chandni Chowk, in the 1980s

the hall has been made into a room with long glass windows and doors. Inside, you can see the book's garlanded bed-like resting place. The time the book is placed here depends on when the chanting finishes; usually between 9 p.m. and 10 p.m. A portion of the banyan tree under which Guru Tegh Bahadur was beheaded is near the Holy Book's night room. It too is behind glass and draped with an orange cloth. However, the holiest place of all is approached down a flight of stairs behind the golden canopy. Here people descend to worship at the original spot where Guru Tegh Bahadur was beheaded.

The Sikh faithful, sitting and listening to the hymns, do so for as long or as little as they wish and you as a visitor are very welcome to join them. Leave the temple by the flight of steps you entered. As you leave you will be offered a little food; a prasad of wheat and ghee cooked together, which is a pleasant mixture called karah prasad.

Walk
8
੧ੳੰ੭

The Guru Ka Langar (The Sikh Communal Kitchen)

At the end of your visit to the worship hall, descend the steps and, facing Chandni Chowk, turn left but don't collect your shoes just yet as you need to be barefoot to enter the communal kitchen, the Guru Ka Langar. Don't leave without visiting this communal kitchen because it shows Sikh community spirit in action. To find it is very easy. Just continue left for a few paces, then turn left through a marble arch back into the gurdwara complex and walk across the courtyard. You'll see a flight of steps in front of you which are guarded by a Sikh wearing white clothing and a blue turban. He has a thick stick which he lifts to let you through or not, if for some reason he feels you shouldn't gain entrance! (Perhaps you've had three meals there already.) Climb the flight of stairs and enter the building in front of you that has a clock above the central arch.

Food is distributed throughout the day and all are welcome. Whatever is received by the gurdwara is cooked and distributed in the kitchen, but the mainstay is dal and chappatis. The kitchen itself is on the right, and this is where you often see people stirring gigantic cauldrons of dal and women sitting cross-legged making chappatis. The dining hall is straight ahead. There are long lengths of matting stretched across the length of the room and diners sit on the mats and await the food which is placed into a metal tray.

In the fifteenth century, when the first Sikh Guru, Guru Nanak, began encouraging people to eat together, he was doing so to try to break down the strict Hindu caste restrictions against inter-dining. In those days, Hindus from different castes never ate together as the higher castes regarded food and drink touched by the lower castes as polluted. Guru Nanak stressed the equality of men, and was strongly opposed to casteism, hence communal kitchens. On an ordinary weekday, about 4,000 meals are served, but on special days the number can rise to 10,000. You can eat as much as you like. There's no virtue attached to taking a small portion but you shouldn't take more than you can eat. The contributions of sacks of flour and lentils are piled up against the wall facing the dining area. Running communal kitchens is an important aspect of Sikhism as they believe individuals should bring food to the gurdwara as though they were contributing to a family party. Everyone contributes and everyone receives.

Anyone of any income group, race, creed, colour or political persuasion can eat here. There is no bar, but there is a wariness of professional beggars, as Sikhism itself upholds the dignity of labour and is against the seeking of alms for survival. If you'd like to read more about Sikhism, turn to the Historical Appendix 'Notes on the Start of Sikhism' at the end of this walk.

At the end of your visit retrace your steps and collect your shoes from the shoe room. Turn left and, still on the marble pavement, you'll pass a small shop selling goods important to Sikhs. The five signs of being a male Sikh are, that you don't cut your hair (kesh), but keep it well-groomed with a comb (kangha);

Walk
8

you wear a circular steel wristband (kara) to remind you of the oneness of God; you carry a dagger (kirppan) to defend your Sikh beliefs; and finally, you don't wear a dhoti because these are difficult to fight in, but wear special cotton undershorts (kacchha). The shop sells four of the five 'k's' in great abundance. The fifth, long hair, one has to provide oneself.

Finding the Sunheri Masjid

Standing outside the shop selling Sikh goods on Chandi Chowk, and with your back to the Red Fort, look ahead and upwards! You can see a golden dome. There are three of them but depending on how tall you are you may not see all three. Walk just a couple of metres along the pavement and cross an alleyway. It's easy to miss the narrow flight of white marble steps up to the mosque as there's nothing to tell you that the mosque is above the shops. The steps up to the mosque are immediately before the shirt shop Silkina. It's a very well-known mosque so do ask shopkeepers if you can't find it.

The Sunheri Masjid (The Golden Mosque)
[Built by Roshan–ud-Dawla Zafar Khan in 1721 and Originally Known by that Name.]

You will not be allowed to enter if you are wearing shorts. Unlike the Jama Masjid, there are no coveralls here so you will be turned away. Entry is also impossible if the mosque is being used for prayers. However, if it isn't being used for worship and you are modestly dressed, climb the steps and cross over to the balcony that faces Chandni Chowk. These days the mosque has been spruced up and there is often a young man around who is willing to explain the significance of this balcony to people who don't have a guidebook.

It is of great historical importance because it was here that Nadir Shah, the Persian king who had defeated the Mughal ruler of the time, Mohammed Shah, sat from 8 a.m. to 3 p.m. on

11 March 1739, and watched his men kill the local citizens in a massacre that left the streets of Delhi littered with corpses. Some estimates say that 30,000 local people were killed by the qizilbash, the Persian soldiers, but others say it was even more. It was a terrible day for the citizenry of Delhi. If you'd like to read about the causes leading up to this grim event turn to the Historical Appendix at the end of Walk 1.

After leaving the mosque, cross over Chandni Chowk. You'll see the shop signs for Siador Saree Kendra next to Titan Watches on the other side, so cross to them when the flow of rickshaws, barrows, motorbikes and cars thins for a minute or two. Hope for a bullock cart. (You can always nip across in front of a bullock cart.) Then turn left and cross to the dry fountain in the middle of the square. This fountain divides the always busy H.C. Sen Marg as it leads to a huge station, Delhi Main, the railway station for Old Delhi.

The Dry Fountain in Bhai Mati Das Chowk

Lord Northbrook contributed money to this typically Victorian fountain and at one time it was called the Northbrook Fountain and for many years after that, the Fountain Chowk (Fountain Square). But all it spouts today is a yellow Sikh pennant. It's been dry for many years. Today, the area is called Bhai Mati Das Chowk and an area of the road near the fountain has been barricaded off in memory of his martyrdom. You can see the man's name, Bhai Mati Das, on posters tied to the fountain; with your back to the fountain, his name can also be found on the Sikh museum named after him, across the left-hand fork of H.C. Sen Marg, directly in line with the fountain. Bhai Mati Das, like Guru Tegh Bahadur, was martyred in an exceptionally cruel way. He was sawn in half lengthwise. To see a dramatic series of paintings of how this was done cross over to the Sikh museum. If in any doubt as to where it is check with the Sikh who is guarding this revered area around the fountain nowadays.

The Sikh Museum

Take off your shoes. In the museum, which is more like a religious art gallery than a place housing ancient objects, make for the last set of paintings in the room next to the exit. The pictures here explain how the Guru revered in the Sisganj Gurdwara (Guru Tegh Bahadur) was forced to watch his fellow Gurus being sawn in half, or wrapped in cotton and set on fire, or boiled alive. Nothing is left to the imagination.

There's so much imprisonment, death and martyrdom associated with this area of Chandni Chowk because it used to be the seventeenth century centre of law and order—the site of the kotwali. (The main police station in Old Delhi is still called the kotwali but has moved up Chandni Chowk.) Any one accused of a crime was held in custody in the kotwali to await trial. It was here too that the dead sons and grandsons of the last Mughal emperor, Bahadur Shah Zafar, (killed by the British officer, Captain Hodson), were displayed in 1857.

Your walk ends here.

Retrace your steps to Chandni Chowk and take a cycle or auto rickshaw back to your car. If you've got here by Metro then cross H.C. Sen Road, take the first turning on your left and follow the flow back to Chandhni Chowk Metro Station.

Walk
8
ੴ

Historical Appendix

Notes on Hinduism

Unlike Christianity, Islam, and Sikhism, Hindusim has no individual founder or fixed starting date. It is a religion with innumerable different strands that have been added over the centuries giving it an appearance of bewildering variety. It is one of the world's oldest religions.

Traces of it, particularly worship of a Shiva-like deity, are found around 2000 BC in the Indus Valley Civilization. The earliest Hindu literature, the Vedas, date from around 1500 BC and are a collection of hymns to various deities, which were composed by the Aryans during their invasions.

The word 'Hindu' is derived from 'Sindhu', the name the Aryans gave to the river Indus where they first settled.

The Aryans were an Indo-European people whose language, Sanskrit, was similar in many ways to classical Greek, and many of whose Gods were similar to the Greek Gods.

As the Aryans settled in India, so their religion absorbed innumerable local cults of the peoples among whom they settled and the numbers of their Gods multiplied.

There was a new phase of Hinduism around 700–500 BC which is reflected in writings called the Upanishads or Vedanta— literally, the 'end' or 'completion' of the Veda.

Philosophers and sages started asking who all these different Gods were and came to the conclusion that there was only one God, one truth and reality, but it manifested itself in many different guises.

They went even further and said that this one ultimate reality of existence existed in all things, including every individual, and that the individual could become one with this reality or Godhead through meditation.

This teaching has remained the cornerstone of Hinduism right up to the present day.

In theory, Hinduism has three main Gods, but in practice most Hindus today would claim to be followers of either Shiva or Vishnu. (Brahma, the creator, has had his role usurped by Shiva, who symbolizes both destruction and recreation.)

Shiva is a wild God, the archetypal ascetic with matted locks and leopard skin loincloth. His sexuality symbolizes a life force which is both creative and destructive, beautiful and ugly. Vishnu is by contrast a more placid and level-headed God, whose role is to preserve things the way they are. His wife Lakshmi symbolizes wealth, prosperity and good luck.

All the Hindu Gods and Goddesses have many stories told

about them, and Hindus worship them in many different ways. The less sophisticated may believe literally in the stories of the God's glorious deeds. But the more well-informed devotees will see the Gods as symbols and representatives of one side of reality: as props to help the simple-minded along the path whose goal, for all Hindus, is to be at one with the ultimate reality of existence; whether it is called Shiva, Vishnu, Allah, or God.

Notes on the Start of Sikhism

The word Sikh is derived from the Sanskrit word 'Shishya' meaning disciple. Sikhs are disciples of their teachers (Gurus), of whom there are ten.

The founder of the faith, Guru Nanak, was born into a learned Punjabi Hindu family in 1469. His family belonged to a caste that was expected to know the Hindu religious books, the Vedas, and his father was the village registrar.

But Nanak also knew about Islam. He grew up with Muslim rulers in power (the Lodis held the Delhi Sultanate), and after he'd finished his basic education he studied Islamic literature and Persian.

Nanak was aware of the tremendous sufferings that wars between Hindus and Muslims had caused for hundreds of years. It was his ambition to bring the two religions together and end the fighting.

Guru Nanak preached that there was only one God, that all humankind were children of that one God and that therefore divisions into Hindus and Muslims were meaningless. He was against idol worship, the existence of mythological beings, formal rituals, the concept of the incarnation of God, and the caste system.

Unlike the teachings of the Hindu Gurus, Guru Nanak encouraged people to find God whilst living responsible family lives as householders. In this respect, Sikhism is similar to Islam. (Hinduism stresses the renunciation of the world and domestic pleasures after a certain age to achieve enlightenment.)

Walk
8
ੴ

Guru Nanak placed the emphasis of his teachings on an awareness of moral values rather than on the performing of ceremonies and rituals. He died a normal death in 1539.

His teachings were continued by his successor Guru Angad—and on Guru Angad's death by Guru Amardas.

Akbar, the Mughal emperor, met Guru Amardas and was impressed by his personality and lack of greed. Akbar helped the new religious community by selling them an area of land in the Punjab. It had a natural pool in the middle of it, which was made into a tank, and around the sides a town developed.

This town was Amritsar and the temple built in the tank itself, which began as a simple building, was magnificently enriched in the nineteenth century. The Golden Temple was built as a Sikh central place of worship—an equivalent to the Muslim Kaba in Mecca.

In 1604, a book compiled by the fifth Guru, Guru Arjan, was placed in the temple in Amritsar. The book was a compilation of the hymns written by the four earlier Gurus, plus those written by five Muslim and ten Hindu saints.

In the eighteenth century, the tenth Guru, Guru Gobind Singh, told his followers that on his death there would be no more men as Gurus. Sikhs had to be guided by the book that Guru Arjan had compiled.

It is now known as the Guru Granth Sahib, contains 5,894 hymns and verses, and is both the source and focus of Sikh worship.

Walk
8
ॐ

Walk **9:**
The Uprising of 1857
(The Indian Mutiny)

The year was 1857 and Delhi was in turmoil. The British East India Company had lost control of the city in May of that year and only recaptured it in September. This walk includes places where the most powerful Brits had their beautiful homes, the army kept its gunpowder and poor soldiers fought long and hard over a swelteringly hot summer. If you plan to walk on a Sunday, bear in mind that the Holy Eucharist will be celebrated at St James' Church at 8.30 a.m. from April to September and from 9 a.m. onwards between October and March and that the Lothian Road Cemetery will be closed. (It is sometimes closed on a Saturday too.)

Places of Interest

THE LOTHIAN ROAD CEMETERY (Open from 9.30 a.m. to 5 p.m. Closed on Sundays.)

THE RUINS OF THE BRITISH MAGAZINE

THE TELEGRAPH MEMORIAL OBELISK

THE OLD RESIDENCY BUILDING (DARA SHIKOH'S LIBRARY) (Open from 9.30 to 6 p.m. Closed on Saturdays and Sundays.)

ST JAMES' CHURCH (Open daily from 9 a.m. to 6 p.m. Holy Eucharist from 8.30 a.m. on Sundays.)

KASHMERE GATE

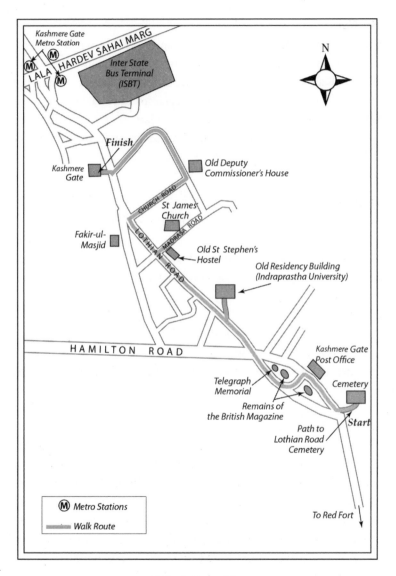

Walk 9: Route Map

Getting There

By Car
Park in the large, well-organized and well-known Red Fort car park in front of the fort's Delhi Gate. It's approached from Nishad Raj Marg. Charges vary according to length of stay but are always reasonable. Then take a cycle or auto rickshaw to the GPO (General Post Office), Kashmere Gate. It's a large white and red painted building. Make sure you are dropped off in front of it. With your back to the post office turn left, and walk downhill towards the bridge.

By Metro
You have a choice. You can either take the Yellow Line to Chandni Chowk or stay on for a further stop and get off at Kashmere Gate. In both cases you will need to take a rickshaw to the start of your walk at the GPO in Lothian Road.

Walk
9
ॐ

The Walk
The entrance gate to the Lothian Road Cemetery is through a small black metal gate which you'll see on the left just before you get to the bridge. If you arrive after 9.30 a.m., it will be unlocked, so enter.

Lothian Road Cemetery
This is an old European cemetery where members of Delhi's Christian community were buried from 1808 to 1867. The most impressive memorial used to be a huge Celtic cross on which was carved a dedication to 'those whose nameless graves lie around' but it collapsed, and now all you can see are large ornately carved chunks of stone amongst the grass. The 'nameless graves' refer to the Europeans who were killed in Delhi at the outbreak of the Great Revolt in May 1857 in the Red Fort itself and around this area. However, most of the individual graves are pre-1857. Explore the cemetery and read some of the inscriptions on the

graves themselves and on the ground. You'll probably come across the small marble slab laid by the distraught parents of Edith May, John and Mary Butler, who felt it important to record even the days of their daughter's short precious life. She died aged one year six months fifteen days. Garnet Byrne, a Sub Inspector of Ordnance, did better. He died at forty-nine.

Parts of the cemetery are in a dishevelled state, as until a few years ago there was a Christian community living here. These Christian squatters built shacks between the graves, sometimes even incorporating them inside their dwellings. It was a real village

Walk
9
౫౷৺৩৪

The Celtic Cross in the 1980s

with thirty-five homes, swept paths, garden plots, a homeopathic physician and the sign of the cross painted in red on front doors. The families were moved out about 2006 as the Archaeological Society of India wished to regain control of the property which the squatters were, of course, damaging. Now hosts of tiny yellow butterflies rise ahead of you when you walk through the long grass and monkeys run along the wall's edge.

When the site was first selected as a cemetery, it had a totally different character. It was a green and tranquil area. This, of course, was long before the railway line was brought to Delhi. The trains started whistling, hooting, and banging in 1868, when the station was opened, and goods and people from the whole of north India started pouring in.

The siting of the railway line so that it effectively cuts Old Delhi into two unequal parts was done deliberately. In other Indian cities this effect was avoided, but here strategic thinking was still affecting planning decisions. The British wanted to be able to get troops into the centre of the city quickly if trouble should ever break out again. The line brought prosperity, yet it destroyed the unity of the old walled city forever.

Leave the cemetery the way you came in.

The Walk to the British Magazine (Gunpowder Store)

The word 'magazine' comes from the Arabic 'maxazin' which means storeroom.

Turn right and walk up the road back towards the GPO; you'll see a red arched structure in the middle of the road, but don't cross to it. This is the first part of the remains of the British Magazine. There's a second part farther up the road. Keep walking for about 100 yards, then in front of the GPO building, cross the road completely, aim for the blue and white tiled urinals, and then, standing on this side of Lothian Road, read the inscriptions above the central arch on the front beneath the mortar. It's difficult to make out the top one but you can guess the British sentiments from the clearly visible newer inscription underneath. This says, 'The persons described as "rebels and mutineers" in the above description were Indian members of the army in the service of the British East India Company trying to overthrow the foreign government.'

The British Magazine

These two gateways are odd structures today in the middle of a busy road as they are obviously remnants from a fortified structure. They are isolated because the large complex to which they belonged was deliberately blown up by the British on 11 May 1857, the day after the sepoys (Indian soldiers) had started their revolt in Meerut. They used to be part of an extensive fortified wall enclosing more buildings in which gunpowder was made and stored. The complex stretched to the river, but it's hard to visualize its former shape these days. All you can do is mentally link the two.

A small group of men blew it up as they were determined that their store of ammunition should not fall into the hands of the rebellious sepoys. The officer in charge, Lieutenant Willoughby, had seen them marching across the bridge earlier that morning. So, with the help of six others he barricaded the outer gates, placed guns inside them and then laid a trail of powder from the store to a tree which stood in the yard of the Magazine. One of the civilian clerks, called Scully, volunteered to stand by the tree and light the fuse when Willoughby gave the signal. The signal came and brave Scully was killed. The others survived, which is very surprising as the explosion was tremendous, the bang being heard 40 miles away in Meerut.

The underlying causes of the Great Revolt were many and complex, but the spark that ignited the uprising was related to fat. The British army had issued new Enfield rifles to their soldiers and told them to load the guns by biting the ends off the cartridges, which was easy to do except that they were greased.

Walk
9
ജ⊙ᘛ

The Hindus worried about the grease being cow fat and the Muslims worried about it being pig fat and so the British top brass had effectively offended most of the Indian soldiers in their army. In Meerut, a town close to Delhi, they mutinied.

This Magazine wasn't the only store of ammunition held by the British in Delhi. In fact, it was the smaller of the two, as the larger had been deliberately sited in an emptier area further away.

The stocks in the larger Magazine were stolen, once the Uprising was underway, by the local people living in the countryside around.

It's not worth crossing to see inside the building. The railings were added to prevent the arches from being used by drug addicts.

Walk a little further along Lothian Road until you are opposite a grey obelisk. This is the Telegraph Memorial. You can easily see it pointing heavenward above the flowery shrubbery.

Walk
9
ཚེ་ལྡན

The Telegraph Memorial
(On the Site of the Wooded Cabin in which the Telegraph Officers Worked)

Although possible, as the small wall has been broken down near the apex of the island, it isn't advisable to cross over to look at the obelisk itself unless you are particularly interested in 1857 memorials. This is because the grass is used as a toilet by rough sleepers and is very dirty and full of rubbish. It's also quite hard to read the inscription itself. However, you can make out 'the electric telegraph has saved India' on its western face. This refers to more events of this fateful May day in 1857. Two signallers, Brendish and Pilkington, had spent the previous day trying to find out why the telegraph lines to Meerut weren't working. They didn't know that the Uprising had broken out and the line cut by the mutinying sepoys. Neither did their officer, Charles Todd; or he wouldn't have set out looking for the fault he thought his juniors had missed.

He never came back. Brendish and Pilkington guessed he'd

been killed because by this time hundreds of people were rushing excitedly past their wooden cabin. As the morning wore on, a wounded British officer shouted at them to keep their doors closed and they could see buildings being set on fire. They knew they had to leave. Before going, Brendish tapped out this message to the British army in the north: 'We must leave office. All the bungalows are being burnt down by the sepoys (Indian soldiers) from Meerut. They came in this morning... Mr Todd is dead I think. He went out this morning and has not returned... We are off.' Thus the British army in Ambala learnt of the uproar in Meerut and Delhi and officers far away from the turbulence could plan counter-attacks. They felt truly grateful to the 'new-fangled' electric telegraph.

Cross back to the opposite side of Lothian Road, walk along a little and cross busy Khela Ghat Marg. You'll be in front of the entrance gate to Ambedkar University, Delhi. Further along you'll see another sign for Guru Gobind Singh Indraprastha University. If you tell the guards you want to visit Dara Shikoh's library they

Walk
9

The Remains of the British Magazine

Sir David Ochterlony an Early Nineteenth-century British Resident at Home with a Hubble-bubble, Musicians and Dancing Girls

will let you in. You'll walk through a pleasant garden towards a large white building you can see in the distance. It has classical columns and intervening wooden shutters.

The Old British Residence
(Traditionally Said to Be Dara Shikoh's Library)
The building you're looking at has very close associations with both Mughal and British ruling elites. The pillars and veranda are British, added about 1803, but behind them is a much older Mughal structure built by Shah Jahan's liberal intellectual son Dara Shikoh in the 1650s. Poor Dara Shikoh was murdered in 1659 by men in the pay of his younger brother Aurangzeb, and his property, including this building (said to be his library), was given to others.

If the building is open then enter through a central doorway above the steps. There's usually a guard. Sometimes, the building is closed; at holiday times the staff, working in the offices inside, are off duty so the building is closed. Assuming that it's not a holiday and the door is open, explore the veranda. You can see the sharp contrast between the cusped arches and pillars of seventeenth century Mughal architecture and the plain columns beloved by the British of the nineteenth century. The British got hold of the building after they'd defeated the Marathas on 11 September 1803, and Sir David Ochterlony made changes when

Walk
9
ఴ౷౸

St Stephen's College Hostel, Lothian Road, in the 1980s

he established a Residency here. He was the first Resident—the most senior British official in Delhi. The work a Resident had to do was amazingly broad. He had to pay the Mughal emperor his pension and generally keep him and his family contented yet powerless, manage political relations between the British government and the many independent local rajas, superintend the administration of the city of Delhi itself and preside over tax collection and the administration of justice. The building was used by many different Residents until 1832 when the job title changed and the first occupant of the new position, called a Civil Commissioner, chose to live elsewhere.

Today, the building is used by the Department of Archaeology, Delhi Administration; and where Dara Shikoh read his lovely handwritten texts, there is a jumble of offices, while on the veranda where British Residents sipped their tea, there are dusty cases of ancient pottery.

Walk
9
ঙৌৰ্ণঙ

Finding St James' Church

Turn right on leaving the university and continue along the Lothian Road. As you walk along this busy road margin, ducking now and again beneath the overhanging bougainvillea, the pavement disappears for a while. Once it reappears you may come across a few pavement dwellers cleaning their pots and guarding their locked wooden boxes especially once past the tree at the crown of the hill. The area is so run down it's almost impossible to believe but in the 1920s this was the smartest European shopping area in Delhi. (Today's Khan Market.) New Delhi hadn't been built and the Civil Lines just to the north was the most exclusive of all the residential areas. If you look at some of the trellis work above the shops, and the shops themselves in the arcade, you can tell they were once very grand and have fallen on hard times. Little did those 1920s shopkeepers know that a hundred years later their trellises would be monkey adventure centres!

Continue walking along the right-hand side of the road.

St James' Church, Engraving Published c. 1838

Just before you reach the church you'll pass a rather strange red building. It looks as though it's a mixture of British barrack architecture and a mosque, as it has the sturdiness of the former with the domes of the latter. It wasn't a barracks and it isn't a mosque but was the hostel to a Christian college, the first in Delhi. The college was opened in 1881, called St Stephen's, and is on the opposite side of the road behind a high wall now the home of the Chief Electoral Officer. Look across and you'll see it. Originally, the teachers at St Stephen's were mostly Englishmen from Cambridge University. This college became highly prestigious and successful and built itself another bigger building, now part of the Delhi University campus. The former hostel, where the students lived, is today part of the Guru Gobind Singh University.

Turn into Madrasa Road on your right. You'll see St James' Church on the left-hand side. It's a large, domed, yellow and white painted church set in a lovely garden. (The madrasa of Madrasa Road was St Stephen's College as the word itself doesn't have solely Muslim connotations.) The main entrance to the church is on the corner at the junction, but these gates are not always open.

To be sure of getting in, keep to the left-hand side and enter by a small metal gate. Buildings used by the ISPK will be on your right. Enter the church by the side door which is immediately in front of you.

St James' Church

Once inside the church, walk towards the stained glass windows behind the altar. Stand facing the altar then walk towards the right to read some of the plaques on the wall to the families killed in the 1857 Uprising. One family, that of Thomas Collins, lost thirty members and the memorial was erected 'by the surviving orphans'. Another to George Beresford's wife and five daughters tells you where they lie buried in the church garden. Later you'll see their graves. They actually died in Chandni Chowk as Mr Beresford was the bank manager of the Delhi Bank there. Their bodies were brought back here.

The man who built the church, and whose first name (James) probably influenced the naming of the church itself (St James) lies buried in front of the altar. Take a seat in his family pew, it's the front row, and read a little about his life.

He was born in 1778, the son of a Scottish soldier, Hercules Skinner, and a Hindu Rajput mother. He had two brothers and three sisters.

He wanted to join the British army but they wouldn't accept him because his mother was an Indian, even though his father was an officer in the Bengal Army. So he became a junior officer, at the age of eighteen, with an Indian chief's forces and fought for him.

It was in 1800, when he was only twenty-two, that he made a vow to build a church. He was badly wounded and had spent two dreadful days in agony lying on a battlefield. A village woman saved his life and the lives of many of his comrades by bringing them bread and water. This is the oft repeated James Skinner tale but as historians point out there isn't any proof!

Later he fought for the great Maratha Chief Sindhia, who ruled large areas of northern and central India at the time. Skinner became an experienced and respected leader. After 1803, when the British forces under General Lake defeated the Maratha forces, Skinner went over to the East India Company army. He made one condition. He'd never fight against the Maharajah of Gwalior, his former master, Sindhia.

Skinner raised cavalry regiments. They were called 'irregular horse' simply because they weren't part of anyone's regular army. He dressed them in yellow, a colour associated with both marriage ceremonies and death in the Rajput tradition. His men were thoroughly trained and Skinner treated them well. They came to be known as Skinner's Horse or the Yellow Boys and won many battles. Their name is still honoured in the Indian army of today but is now used for an armoured regiment. The church itself has a military feel to it with its Skinner's Horse Gallery in a side passage and lists of Skinner's Horse Commanding Officers near the altar. Don't miss the two slim lances with their black and yellow Skinner's Horse pennants tied to the columns opposite the main entrance door of the church. If you've read William Dalrymple's *The Last Mughal* and know the characters living here at the time of the Uprising don't miss the photograph of the Reverend Jennings, the influential Evangelical, hanging on the wall in the gallery. Before you leave the church for the sunshine outside, look at the beautiful marble slab on the floor in front of the altar near to Col. Skinner's grave. The white marble is inlaid with the browns and greens of a weeping plant. The text beneath explains why it's there and mentions the name of William Fraser. Remember the name!

The Skinner Family Graves

Leave the church through the Skinner's Horse Gallery door, turn left and walk along the path round the back of the church to visit the group of graves within the railings. There's a gate in the railings on the side furthest from the church. They're all members of Skinner's family but certainly not all the members. Although James Skinner was baptized a Christian, his personal life was that of a wealthy, respectable, early nineteenth century gentleman. When he died, it was said that sixty-four men claimed they were his sons and had the right to inherit property from his estate. Perhaps some 'sons' were impostors, but James Skinner did keep a zenana (a harem) of Indian women. As you wander around the graves you can see how some deaths are recorded in both English and Persian. English was the new up and coming language in the region at the time, whereas Persian had held sway for hundreds of years. Colonel Skinner's house was near to the church on the other side of the main road. He was a hospitable man, fond of giving lively parties to which lovely dancing girls were invited, as was the custom at the time, to graciously entertain his Indian and European guests. He was a very well-loved man in Delhi.

Walk
9
སྱ⟨ᠪ⟩ᢒᠪ

Leave the Skinner graves and with your back to the church turn left and walk towards the main road. Aim for the large memorial cross, but before you reach it look at the grave of William Fraser which is immediately in front. The inscription records his murder. In 1835, when he was killed, he was an extremely important man as he held the post of British Commissioner—the most senior British position at the time. The original beautiful marble grave was destroyed during the Uprising as the church was the scene of heavy bombardment. You will remember having seen an elegant fragment in the church in front of the altar.

William Fraser's Death

His death had nothing to do with the mutinous sepoys. It occurred long before the mutiny, and the man who organized Fraser's death was not a poor soldier but a wealthy Muslim nobleman, Nawab Shams-ud-din Khan.

The young lord had known Fraser all his life but had grown to hate him. The reasons for this intense dislike were multiple.

After the Indian nobleman's father died there was trouble over the inheritance of land between the young lord and his two brothers. Fraser never took the young lord's side. That was one reason. A second concerned the young lord's beautiful sister. William Fraser liked women and the Nawab suspected that Fraser intended to seduce her. Finally the Nawab's pride was insulted. He went to call on Fraser but was turned away. This was too much; so he decided to have Fraser murdered. He succeeded on 22 March when a man he employed shot Fraser at point-blank range as he was returning home after a party. Nawab Shams-ud-din Khan was hanged on 3 October 1835, as was the man who had actually fired the shot. There was another accomplice but he saved his skin by giving evidence against them. The original grave to William Fraser was a beautiful marble one, but it was destroyed during the Great Revolt.

The Memorial Cross

Walk behind Fraser's grave and take a look at this plain memorial cross. George Beresford's family are buried here with many others. Look at the inscriptions around the lower part of the pedestal in English (facing the church), Sanskrit (facing the road), Urdu (facing the entrance gate) and Farsi (facing Church Road). The people of the time wanted to make sure absolutely everybody knew they were immortalizing the Christian dead slain during the Uprising of 1857.

If you would like to know more about Col. Skinner and his church you can buy a booklet *A Living Witness* from the church attendant.

The Deputy Commissioner's House

On leaving the church, walk to the main road (Lothian Road) and then turn right, pass a bus shelter, and at the first road you come to, turn right. It's Church Road. It has car parts shops, mechanics and a little Hindu shrine. You'll see a large domed building at

Kashmere Gate c. 1860. Photographer: Possibly Beato

the bottom of the road which now houses the offices of the Northern Railway. But it wasn't built for railway administration! It had far greater pretensions to grandeur as it was the British Deputy Commissioner's house the second most important British Civil Servant in Delhi in the late nineteenth century. New, plain, modern buildings have seriously encroached on the garden that used to spread out so magnificently from the house to the road, but the building's lovely dome hints at its former glory.

With your back towards the Railway Offices, turn right and follow the road round to meet the main road again. Look across it and you'll see the double arches of Kashmere Gate. Cross to them; there are gaps in the metal road dividers to nip through and stone benches in front of the arches where you can rest and read a little.

The Kashmere Gate

This northern entrance to Shahjahanabad is the only one that ever had two openings. Royal processions left Delhi here, taking Mughal royalty to spend summers in Kashmir. To the British this area is of particular interest. It was the scene of desperate fighting on 14 September 1857, when British forces attacked the city, determined to take it back from the sepoys, the Indian soldiers of the Uprising. The city wall had been breached by a tremendous cannonade from British guns which had bombarded the area from the ridge behind. About 8,000 men had been mustered on the ridge to attack the city but many were ill. One of the brigadiers (Wilson) maintained the night before the assault, that only 4,500 were fit enough to fight. It worried him terribly.

Opposing them was a much larger force of freedom fighters, only they were beset with problems. (It has been estimated that there were upwards of 30,000 sepoys in the city in July, plus another 25,000 untrained but fervent Muslim fighters armed with axes. By August, the number of sepoys is thought to have fallen to about 20,000.) The sepoys had asked the emperor for his support and he'd agreed, but at the highest levels there were disagreements about who was in charge of the different regiments of the sepoy army—royal princes or experienced commanders—and as well as the loss through casualties, many groups of soldiers simply deserted as they were starving. There was a desperate shortage of food in the city, after such a huge influx of soldiers, and water was scarce too as the British had prevented water from the Yamuna Canal flowing into the city. They'd also run out of captured gunpowder and were making their own, which wasn't as effective, and there was a shortage of gunpowder caps.

The British forces, although better fed and well supplied with armaments, had a huge task ahead of them. The cannonade had made gaps in the walls but still they had to cross a 20-foot ditch before trying to scale the gaps with ladders whilst being shot at constantly. There was tremendous confusion and hundreds were shot or fell onto bayonets. The losses were so heavy that although the British did get through, one of the brigadiers in charge seriously considered retreating to the camp on the ridge his men had left a few days earlier. But he didn't. After six days of desperate hand-to-hand fighting in the streets of the city, Delhi was back under British control. (If you'd like to read more about the events of 1857, get hold of William Dalrymple's *The Last Mughal*, for a blow-by-blow account.)

With your back to the Lothian Road, you'll see two modern explanatory signs on the left; walk to an older memorial stone tablet at the rear of the arch. It is inscribed with the names of the crucial, but small, party of soldiers who died here while placing sacks of gunpowder to blow in the gates. The main thrust of the British forces followed, spread out through the city, and they eventually regained control.

The tablet gives a wrong impression. It lists so few names and yet hundreds died attacking this gate. Walk back a little. You can still see the cannonball marks.

Your walk ends here.

Take a rickshaw back to your car or walk to the Kashmere Gate Metro Station which is immediately to your left.

Walk
9
ೞ☉☎

Walk **10:**
Civilian Calm

Where the British used to hold their parties, have their bungalows, play tennis and be buried. This is a quiet walk and a complete contrast to the hustle and bustle of the other nine. There are no rickshaws in these leafy lanes and you can stroll around, talking to the friend by your side, quite easily. However, this is the longest of the walks and if you'd like to make it shorter, omit the Nicholson Cemetery.

Places of Interest

OBEROI MAIDENS HOTEL
THE CIVIL LINES
MOTHER TERESA'S ORPHANAGE
THE PARK QUDSIA BAGH
THE NICHOLSON CEMETERY

Getting There

By Car

Park in the car park of Oberoi Maidens Hotel on Sham Nath Marg. To get there you can either drive through Old Delhi itself, past the Red Fort, Kashmere Gate, the ISBT and the Ring Road, or avoid the old city by approaching via the Ring Road (Mahatma Gandhi Road) and turning left up Yamuna Marg, then right for a few hundred metres until you see the hotel on your

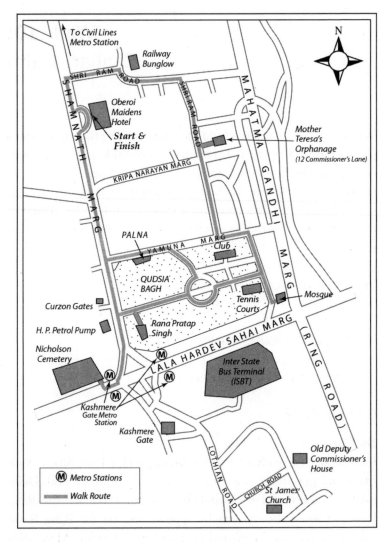

Walk 10: Route Map

right. Turn in and park. Don't enter the hotel itself. You start
this walk in the grounds of the Maidens Hotel. With your back
to the road, walk along the left side of the hotel to the gardens
behind and find a shady spot to read about the Civil Lines and
Mr Joseph Maiden.

By Metro
Take the Yellow Line and get off at the Civil Lines station and exit
to the street Sham Nath Marg. Stand facing the road and walk
left down Sham Nath Marg, crossing Sri Ram Road before you
reach Maidens Hotel. Security guards looking very like London
Metropolitan policemen will check that you're not a security
risk, then let you through into the hotel grounds. Don't enter
the hotel itself. With your back to the road, walk along the left
side of Maidens Hotel to the gardens behind and find a shady
spot to read about the Civil Lines.

The Civil Lines

Walk
10
ॐ☉ॐ

Today, the district known as the Civil Lines is a pleasant north
Delhi residential area. A hundred years ago it was a suburb with
a difference, for in those days virtually all the inhabitants were
British, involved in administering an empire on which they
thought the sun would never set. After the Great Revolt of 1857,
many Europeans felt nervous of living amongst Indian people
within the city walls as memories of the massacres of European
families near Kashmere Gate lingered long. So they built their
houses in the wilderness to the north.

Wealthy Indians who owned land here, and could have built
houses themselves, were absolutely amazed at Europeans choosing
to live in an area they thought quite beyond the pale. They
despised a 'rural' existence; only the cultured city life, with its
sophisticated evenings spent listening to poetry or music appealed.

So, from the 1860s onwards, single-storey houses were built
in huge enclosures all over this area. Each house was guarded by

watchmen recruited locally from the pastoral community known as Gujar. It was absolutely essential to have a Gujar watchman, for if you didn't, you were immediately robbed.

These houses were called bungalows. The word, so familiar to everyone these days, has an interesting history. It derives from Banga, the Bengali word for Bengal itself. In Hindustani, anything deriving from Bengal was said to be 'bangla'. So from 'Banga' to 'bangla' to bungalow to reach the word used to describe a style of house common in Bengal. This type of house was based on the simple hut of the Bengali peasant but enlarged and adapted for Europeans living in India. Two of its most important features were that it was only one storey high and was covered by a large thatched roof that was continued beyond the walls to provide shady verandas. The basic plan was simple: a large central area which acted as a dining and sitting room with bedrooms at each corner.

Walk
10
ཚ⊙ⲟ

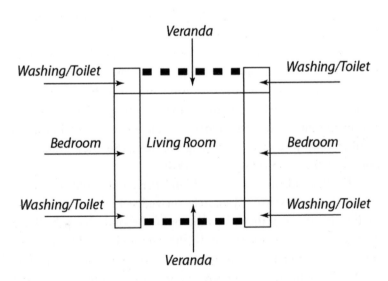

Ground Plan of an Eighteenth-century Bungalow

By the late nineteenth century, Europeans were applying the word bungalow to all sorts of houses—many often made in brick—and the thatched roof replaced by tile.

A bungalow came to mean anything that wasn't a mansion. The families who lived in the bungalows of Delhi's Civil Lines had a very high opinion of themselves. From the 1860s to the 1880s, the group had been almost entirely administrative mostly members of the prestigious Indian Civil Service. Then in the 1890s, more 'ordinary' people such as mill and railway managers began to build their bungalows here. The administrators were terribly worried that the quality of the Civil Lines was being diluted by the entry of 'second-class' Englishmen and complained bitterly about it.

Indian families only began to build here in any numbers in the twentieth century. In 1905, there was an outbreak of plague within the walled city and this lessened the prejudice against living in the suburbs.

Walk
10
ఞ⊙ఇ

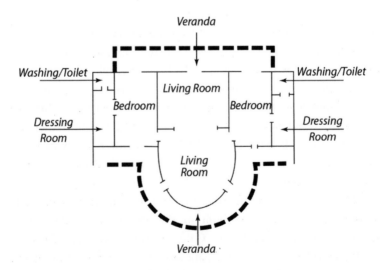

Ground Plan of a Late Nineteenth-century Bungalow

When Delhi took over from Calcutta as India's capital in 1912, building in the Civil Lines really boomed. The district retained its reputation as being the best of Delhi's residential areas until New Delhi was built and government officials were moved south of the Viceregal Lodge to live graciously in the new bungalows lining the wide tree-lined roads.

Mr Joseph Maiden and Oberoi Maidens Hotel

The Oberoi Hotel Group took over Maidens in 1943, but the hotel was built long before that and here at the back of the hotel it is very clear to see. Turn to face the hotel. There's a swimming pool behind you on your left. It's beautifully located with a banana tree near the water.

Now with the swimming pool to your left and behind you, look at the right-hand wing of the building which encloses the terrace restaurant and a grassy courtyard. It is part of the original Maiden's Metropolitan Hotel with its turn-of-the-century pointed arches and small curved windows above. Mr Joseph Maiden built his hotel in 1890. He was a most successful hotelier and went on to build a second storey and enlarge his hotel considerably over the following years. You can see how the central portion of the hotel towers over its side wings. His hotel was full to overflowing during the Delhi Durbar of 1903 as it was *the* place to stay; Delhi's answer to the Ritz! Mr Maiden was born into a humble family in New Ferry, near Birkenhead, in 1867 and his father was a journeyman plasterer. Joseph Maiden ran other hotels in Delhi before building his own but he may originally have arrived in India as a soldier.

His hotel wasn't the first to cater to the European trade as there had been hotels built in the 1830s and 1840s within the city walls near Kashmere Gate. However, after the Uprising of 1857 and the dramatic separation of the British and Indian communities, new hotels were only built in the Civil Lines.

Edward Lutyens, the architect of Rashtrapati Bhavan (in his

Walk
10
ৡৢ৾ৣ৾৶

day called the Viceregal Lodge), lived here while supervising the Bhavan's construction and the twenty-seven-year-old Edward, Prince of Wales, was given a grand ball in the hotel when in Delhi as part of a tour of the empire. At the time, Civil Lines society bubbled with excitement at having the prince among them, but perhaps their welcome would have been more muted if they'd known how things would turn out (later) after the prince's meeting with Mrs Wallis Simpson and his abdication of the throne to marry her.

Walk to the front of the hotel.

The large wood and glass windows and doors in between the columns of the ground floor are 1950 additions needed to keep in the cooled air once air conditioning had been installed. Originally it was a shady veranda where guests could sit sipping their gin and tonics before dinner.

And finally...it's said that two young women who were staying at Maidens found out rather unpleasantly that their holiday was costing more than they had budgeted for. They telegrammed their parents thus: 'Send money or maidens no longer'.

The Walk to Qudsia Bagh

Leave the grounds of the hotel. Stand with your back to the front of the hotel and leave by walking out of the exit on your right. Turn right and prepare to walk about 200 metres to Shri Ram Road. You might notice that this wide road has an identity crisis, because on the left-hand side of the street are the Alipur Estate Apartments which are at 10 Alipur Road whilst opposite is a private house addressed as 9 Sham Nath Marg. This is because Sham Nath Marg is the present day name supplanting the old name of Alipur Road which was a plain name, but a good one, as the road leads to Alipur village. Mr Sham Nath was mayor of Delhi for two years from 1960 to 1962. This Civil Lines area is confusing in terms of street names as they often have two, while some streets even have the same name although going in different directions!

It's difficult to see the houses on the right on Sham Nath Marg these days as high walls hide them from view. Yet there is one house you can glimpse from the pavement on the right-hand side and that's a property now used by the Delhi Police Officers Mess. It has typical Civil Lines features: low building with a veranda, painted in a light colour and standing in a large garden. Take a look as you pass the wide second gate belonging to the Police Officers Mess. It's usually open and always guarded so don't arouse too much interest! It's not surprising that these houses have been bought by institutions as they need a large staff to keep going which wasn't a problem in the 1870s.

At the first road you come to on the right, turn right into Shri Ram Road. (Consult your map on page 162.)

Shri Ram Road

Walk
10

Once you've turned right you'll see the name of this road in Hindi and English on a post near the restaurant Mochar. It's usually a quiet, pleasant road but there isn't a pavement so be wary of cars.

Walk along for about 200 metres until you come to the gateway to Railway Building No. 34 A, 34 C and D.K. Pandey. It's a large, red brick, late nineteenth century building originally built for one British family, the railway manager, his wife and children. Yes, those despised diluters of nineteenth century Civil Lines purity lived here!

Now, as the names on the signposts indicate, it has been divided up into many dwellings. As you stand facing the bulk of the main house, look left down a side lane. You'll see a row of small buildings that look like segments of tunnels. Today, each is used as a home, and an air conditioner protrudes proudly from each rear wall, but they were most probably built for stores or stabling animals.

The road makes a dog-leg turn so follow it round and continue along Shri Ram Road. The area has retained its historical link with the railway as it is known as Railway Colony and you'll see a sign 11-A (Railways) 34-B on one side of a gate on your left. Further along, you'll pass a once elegant house Hari Saden that has fallen into disrepair.

Turn right about 100 metres further on, opposite a gated road. The high black metal gates are usually closed but aren't always, so be aware that you may see them pushed to the sides. After turning right, you'll pass some small shops and a dry-cleaners on the left. Although you may feel that you are leaving Shri Ram Marg the further you go on, shop addresses indicate that you aren't. This often happens in Delhi. Roads twist and turn and yet keep their names. Continue to walk along and you'll have to walk through a very narrow metal gateway. The metal gate is open from 5 a.m. to 11 p.m. On the other side of this gate Shri Ram Marg changes to Commissioner's Lane. Turn left at the first lane entering from the left beyond the metal gateway. It'll take you to the orphanage. Once you've turned, you'll see the sign for Mother Teresa's Orphanage on the wall.

Walk
10
ॐॐॐ

Mother Teresa's Orphanage (12, Commissioner's Lane)

The orphanage is open to visitors from 9 a.m. to 4 p.m., and the Sisters are very welcoming. There are between fifty and sixty children at this orphanage from tiny babies to six-year-olds. The children have an afternoon rest between 12 and 3 p.m. If you call outside these hours you can be shown round the building as the children are studying or playing. As these children are being prepared for adoption the Sisters are keen to improve the children's social skills and as soon as they are old enough they are enrolled in nursery schools. If the orphanage seems quieter than you expected, this is why! If the children are resting, a Little Sister of Charity will sit with you in an airy lobby and explain their work and how the orphanage survives. Donations are the key, whether of money or food. People who visit often leave monetary donations which are really appreciated as they can be used to buy medicine and the orphanage often receives gifts of clothing and food such as rice and dal and fruit. Some families celebrate a child's birthday or a wedding anniversary by holding the party here and sharing the happiness and special food of the day with the children. The first orphanage on this site was opened in 1952 in an ordinary Commissioner's Lane house. The much newer orphanage that you see in front of you now was opened in 2006 and all agree that it suits their needs much better!

Leave the orphanage, retrace your steps and turn left at the first junction. Walk along this continuation of Commissioner's Lane, and when this lane meets another, you'll face a house named Shikhar 7-A. Turn left. You follow the road round the bend and will be walking slightly downhill. As soon as you are round the bend you are in Raj Narain Road. Walk 200 metres till you reach a main road (Yamuna Marg) and you'll face the trees and railings of a park. This park is Qudsia Bagh; the park you want. The park entrance gate is about a 100 metres to your left on the other side of the road. Enter the park.

Walk
10
ॐ☙

Qudsia Bagh
(Gardens Built by the Dowager Queen Qudsia in 1748)

There's an unceasing background roar of the traffic from the Ring Road, yet it's an attractive, shady park open to everyone and particularly appreciated at lunchtime when people come here for a break. In spite of its nearness to the Ring Road, it's still surprisingly peaceful and a haven for wildlife. There are lots of birds here, especially red kites, green parakeets and mynahs, as well as the occasional peacock, hundreds of little squirrels and even the odd mongoose.

Pleasant though it is, the park you see today is a pale shadow of the magnificence the Dowager Queen Qudsia knew in the eighteenth century. Her highly exclusive park contained a palace, a mosque, a summer house, canals, waterfalls, rose gardens and many fruit trees. In those days, her park stretched down to the banks of the Yamuna and one entered through magnificent gateways. There's one left and you'll see it as the walk unfolds.

The palace itself has completely disappeared but we know what it looked like as there is a beautiful picture entitled 'Cotsea Bhaug' by those tough, prolific and talented eighteenth century English artists, Thomas and William Daniell. They arrived in Delhi in 1789 so the palace was only about forty years old in their painting.

Qudsia Begum began life not as a noble lady but a dancing girl. She charmed her way into the heart of the Mughal Emperor Mohammed Shah, and their son Ahmed Shah became emperor on his father's death in 1748.

Just like her late husband, Qudsia was a pleasure loving and extravagant person. Her husband had been pleasure loving to the point of disaster. He was the emperor who had been defeated by the Persians, seen 30,000 of his Delhi citizenry slaughtered and watched as the victorious army packed up his Peacock Throne and trundled it back to Persia.

Walk
10
ఴఠఴ

Continue walking straight ahead. There are many trees masking the mosque, but eventually you'll see the domes of Qudsia Begum's mosque on your left and soon reach a red Archaeological Society of India post for 'Qudsiya Masjid'. The mosque, although just a ruin, is still in use for worship and carefully looked after with rows of potted plants adding greenery to the old brick walls. There's an ablutions tank in front of the mosque, now dry, with more plants resting on its ledges. The water needed for ritual washing is supplied by a row of taps. This whole area was severely damaged in 1857 as it was in the direct line of fire from the Indian soldiers (sepoys), who had captured and were now defending Delhi, and the attacking British forces pounding the area from the ridge. Restoration work is in progress.

Retrace your steps, and as you come across some tennis courts, turn left; the courts are, however, hard to see through the foliage. These belong to the Masonic Club. After turning left

The Old Gateway in Qudsia Bagh

you can see the red clay of the courts through the foliage. They don't play on grass in Delhi! However, there's a large grassy area opposite used for wedding tents when offspring of club members marry. The white building on your right is the Masonic Club itself. This is for members only and has a restaurant, a bar, a card room, a billiards room and a lounge.

This park has a distinctive British air about it. Perhaps it's the tennis courts, the curving paths, and the club, or perhaps because an English gardener, Mr Smith, was employed to reorganize the garden and bring back the beauty that the fighting had destroyed. He knew a European kind of beauty. Qudsia's traditional Persian style of garden based on formal patterns of squares (char bagh), filled with fruit trees and flowers, and divided by water channels and fountains gradually disappeared under tennis courts and lawns.

It's strange to think that at one time apartheid was in operation here. Indian people could use the gardens in the mornings as they crossed it to the bathing ghats on the Yamuna river bank. The afternoons were reserved by the Europeans for tennis.

The path passes under all that remains of Qudsia Begum's imposing western gateway the main entrance to her pleasure garden and palace.

Walk on for about 150 metres beyond the gateway, aiming for a row of red and white bollards, and you'll see a colossal statue of a mounted warrior on your left. He's Rana Pratap Singh. He used to be up high on a pedestal shaped like a hill. Sadly, the Delhi Metro Project has cut him down to a standard, more modest one. Find a shady seat (they're in the form of concrete mushrooms here) and read a little about this wonderfully bewhiskered military hero.

Rana Pratap Singh
[Sixteenth Century Ruler of Mewar, an Old Kingdom Now a Part of Rajasthan]
This statue was erected in 1976. The man it commemorates is a hero because he never bowed to the great power of the Muslim

Emperor Akbar. The Hindu Rana ruled an area in Rajasthan that modern Udaipur now falls within. The Rana is mounted on Chetak, his famous warhorse: 'Chetak' means 'Speedy'.

Akbar was determined that the Rana would pay him homage and used force to bring it about. Akbar's forces used elephants against the Rana's troops and when the Rana was in hiding chased him from hilltop to hilltop, but he was never caught.

Finally, Akbar had to call his army away to fight in the north and the Rana regained his kingdom. He ruled for twenty-five years and died at the age of fifty-one.

Approaches to the Nicholson Cemetery

(1) If the Delhi Metro Rail Corporation has completed this stretch of the underground and taken its barriers down, leave the park through the gate on the left opening into Sham Nath Marg, cross over the road and walk downhill to the Ring Road (Mahatma Gandhi Marg). Follow the pavement round to the right. As there are many bus stops here there are also many people waiting around, spilling into the road and eating. There is an amazingly wide variety of snack stalls and fruit barrows catering to the needs of peckish passengers. Negotiate them all and you'll soon come to the large red entrance arch of the Nicholson Cemetery.

(2) If the park exit is still closed off, retrace your steps and take the first path on your left which will lead you through a yellow barrier out of the park and into Yamuna Road once again. Turn left. As you walk along Yamuna Road you'll notice a wicker cot set into an alcove in the wall on the left. This cot has been placed here by the Delhi Council for Child Welfare (DCCW) and the home itself is called Palna which means cradle. A desperate mother can place a baby in it, secretly at night, and the baby will be taken in, cared for and then adopted. Between one and two babies are placed here every month. Adoption is a very carefully controlled process in India and can take between one and two years. Visitors willing to make a donation are welcome to call in.

British gardening enthusiasts might be particularly interested in calling as one corner of the garden here was the focus of a television gardening programme. It was featured in 'Ground Force in India' with Alan Titchmarsh and Charlie Dimmock. They created a pleasant area for the children to enjoy with plants, paths and of course several trademark Charlie Dimmock water features. Sadly the water feature looks pretty dry these days.

At the T junction of Yamuna Marg and Sham Nath Marg, cross over the road, turn left and walk in the direction of the HP Garage. Walk downhill towards the Ring Road (Lala Hardev Sahai Marg). There isn't much pavement here but follow the road round to the right. Once again, as there are many bus stops here there are also many people waiting around, spilling into the road and eating. There is an amazingly wide variety of snack stalls and fruit barrows catering to the passengers. Negotiate them all and once round the bend you'll soon come to the large red entrance arch of the Nicholson Cemetery.

Walk
10

The Nicholson Cemetery

Push the gate open, but if the gate is fastened from the inside, knock and someone will open it. Don't be put off by the caretaker's yappy dogs! The caretaker, his wife or their children may come to meet you but do enter even if no one seems to be around. It's a fascinating place to explore and a good one for seeing monkeys as they enjoy the trees and wildness here. They emerge silently from behind gravestones and certainly have no fear of the living or the dead. They tend to congregate on the left-hand side of the cemetery and at the back. If you dislike monkeys, keep over to the right and stay near the caretaker's family house near the front.

The epitaphs say so much about the people of the period. You can learn about the diseases that killed them (TB, for instance, wiped out one complete family very quickly), but also about their attitudes. For example, the son who didn't write his mother's name on her tomb—just his own and this touching poem.

'Passing Stranger call this not
A place of dreary gloom.
I love to linger near this spot
It is my beloved mother's tomb.'

As you wander about you'll find many who died as infants; there are heartbreaking epitaphs to the loss of 'little angels or little lambs' who were 'born on earth but bloomed in heaven' as cholera and other diseases took a heavy toll. Yet it was lightning that took the life of poor James Cummins, the Telegraph Master, who left a wife and child 'bewailing his loss'. Some graves give the place of birth through phrases like: 'Born in Welshpool 1815, died in Delhi 1865', whilst two others are dedicated to missionaries with epitaphs in English and Urdu.

There is a shortage of Christian burial sites in Delhi and no more new graves are allowed to be dug here. The only recent burials allowed to take place here are to Christian Indian families, either Protestant or Catholic, with long standing family graves in the cemetery. Yet even so, there are complications. A family is only allowed two bodies in a grave at any one time, so after about ten years the bones of one are usually removed and put in a niche so that another body-bearing coffin can be added later. Such is the shortage of Christian burial sites that the Roman Catholic Church in India allows for cremation.

Before leaving, take a look at the grave of the man who gave his name to the cemetery, Brigadier General John Nicholson.

Brigadier General John Nicholson's Grave

Nicholson's grave is easy to find. It's just on the right of the main entrance along a path going up a slight rise. It is surrounded by tall railings. Nicholson was crucial to the success of the British attack on Delhi which regained the city from the Indian sepoys and their supporters, who had taken it over in May 1857. He ended their control in September of the same year. He died as a result of wounds received in this attack.

The man, Nicholson, was tall and bearded and his manner haughty and rather cold. He spoke little. Before arriving here to control the British troops he'd worked in the Punjab where he stamped out lawlessness quite ruthlessly. It's known that he pursued criminals personally and displayed a criminal's severed head on his desk. But he was a very good general, concerned about the welfare of his men and brave to the point of foolhardiness.

He died as a result of being shot in the back whilst leading an attack on Delhi's Lahore Gate, which no longer exists, but was a western gate. He took ten days to die. During this period of his decline fierce fighting was going on throughout the city as British soldiers forced their way, street by street, southwards from Kashmere Gate. Their losses were so great that another British brigadier called Wilson, who considered calling the whole thing off and retreating to the safety of the camp on the ridge, left several days before.

Nicholson, although dying, heard this (and was furious) and said that he thanked God he still had the strength to shoot Wilson if necessary.

Walk
10
༃᠖ᢙ

The Nicholson Cemetery

The Walk Back to Oberoi Maidens Hotel

Leave the emptiness of the cemetery and rejoin the noise and crush of the Ring Road. Retrace your steps. Walk round the corner and pass the HP petrol station on Sham Nath Marg, but when you come to the Oberoi Apartments, pause and look at the huge metal gates.

The gates have 'Curzon House 1903' emblazoned on the front. They obviously belong to an earlier period than the modern dwellings you can see in the distance. The older building was demolished long ago, but it was originally built to house British officials administering the Delhi Durbar of 1903. It was called Curzon House out of respect for the British Viceroy of the time. Lord Curzon never lived here.

The Oberoi Maidens Hotel is on the opposite side of this road a little farther along.

Your walk ends here.

The Oberoi Maidens Hotel coffee shop is open from 7 a.m. to 10 p.m. It's a pleasant place to relax with a cool drink and cool air conditioning after your walk. This hotel is one of the nicest places to stay in Old Delhi. It manages to combine the old world charm and dignity appropriate to a heritage building with the provision of everything a modern visitor could want. Unfortunately, it is only for those with deep pockets.

Walk
10
ॐ☙☙ॐ

Further Reading

Four books formed the core of our reading on Delhi and were constantly consulted. Information from these titles appears in almost every walk, so to prevent repetition they have been listed separately.

Dayal, Maheshwar, *Rediscovering Delhi: The Story of Shahjahanabad*, 2nd edition, S. Chand and Co. Ltd., Delhi, 1982.

Gupta, Narayani, *Delhi between Two Empires 1803-1931: Society, Government and Urban Growth,* Oxford University Press, Delhi, 1981.

Kaul, H.K., ed., *Historic Delhi: An Anthology,* Oxford University Press, Delhi, 1985.

Sharma, Y.D., *Delhi and Its Neighbourhood,* 2nd edition, Director General, Archaeological Survey of India, New Delhi, 1974.

Further reading relating to specific walks:

WALK 1: The Red Fort

Crowe, S. and S. Haywood, *The Gardens of Mughal India: A History and a Guide,* Vikas Publishing House Pvt. Ltd., Delhi, 1983.

Blake, Stephen P., 'Cityscape of an Imperial Capital: Shahjahanabad in 1739', in Frykenberg, R.E., ed., *Delhi Through the Ages: Essays in Urban History, Culture and Society,* Oxford University Press, Delhi, 1986.

Gascoigne, Bamber, *The Great Moghuls,* Time Books International, New Delhi, 1971.

Kaye, M.M., ed., *The Golden Calm: An English Lady's Life in Moghul Delhi,* Webb and Bower (Publishers) Limited, London, 1980.

WALK 2: The Jama Masjid

Dube, D.N. and Pramodini Varma, *Delhi and its Monuments,* Spantech Publishers Pvt. Ltd., New Delhi, 1987.

Michel, George, ed., *Architecture of the Islamic World: Its History and Social Meaning,* Thames and Hudson, London, 1978.

Sen, S.P., *Dictionary of National Biography* (four volumes), Institute of Historical Studies, Calcutta, 1972.

WALK 3: Wings and Weddings

Thomas, R., *Hindu Religion, Customs and Manners,* D.B. Taraporevala Sons and Co. Private Limited, Bombay, 6th edition, 1975.

Lai, Premila, *Premila Lai's Indian Recipes,* Calcutta, Rupa & Company, 1974.

Sarkar, S.N., *Keeper of Delhi's "Sweet" Tradition: The Legend of Ghantewala, Sulabh India,* Sulabh India, New Delhi, 1987.

Hankin, Nigel, *Hanklin Janklin or a Stranger's Rumble Tumble Guide to Some Words, Customs and Quiddities Indian and Indo British,* Banyan Books, New Delhi, 1992.

Peck, Lucy, *Delhi: A Thousand Years of Building,* Roli Books, New Delhi, 2005.

WALK 4: Walled City Gateways

Prasad, L. and U. Sharma, *A Simple History of Medieval India, AD 1000-1707,* Lakshmi Narain Agarwal (Educational Publishers) Agra.

Varma, P. K. and Shankar S., *Havelis of Old Delhi,* Bookwise (India) PVT. Ltd., Delhi, 1992.

WALK 5: Massage and Market Streets

Sen, S.P., *Dictionary of National Biography* (four volumes), Institute of Historical Studies, Calcutta, 1972.

Jaffrey Madhur, *An Invitation to Indian Cooking,* Penguin Books, London, 1978.

WALK 6: Spices, Nuts and Pickles

Spear, Percival, *Twilight of the Mughals: Studies in Late Mughal Delhi,* Oriental Books Reprint Corporation, New Delhi, 1969.

Upton, E., *The D.C.W.A. Cookery Book: With Household and Cookery Hints, Gardening Notes and Miscellaneous Information,* 2nd edition, The Delhi Commonwealth Women's Association, New Delhi, 1976.

Varma, P. K. and Shankar S., *Havelis of Old Delhi,* Bookwise (India) PVT. Ltd., Delhi, 1992.

WALK 7: Sadhus and Trains

Banerji, Brojendranath, *Begum Samru,* M.C. Sarkar and Sons, Calcutta, 1925.

Thomas, P., *Hindu Religion, Customs and Manners,* 6th edition, D.B. Taraporevala Sons and Co. Private Ltd., Bombay, 1975.

WALK 8: Spiritual Chandni Chowk

Singh, Daljit and Angela Smith, *The Sikh World,* Religions of the World Series, Macdonald and Company, London, 1985.

Sivananda, Swami, *Hindu Fasts and Festivals,* 4th edition, The Divine Life Society, Shivanandanagar, 1983.

WALK 9: The Great Revolt

Hibbert, Christopher, *The Great Mutiny: India 1857,* Penguin Books, London, 1980.

Ramesh, Indira, 'Sahib James Skinner', in *The India Magazine,* Volume 7, March 1987.

Dalrymple, William, *The Last Mughal,* Penguin Books, New Delhi, 2006.

WALK 10: Civilian Calm

King, Anthony D., *The Bungalow: The Production of a Global Culture,* Routledge and Kegan Paul, London, 1984.

Hibbert, Christopher, *The Great Mutiny: India 1857,* Penguin Books, London, 1980.

Acknowledgements

As with the first and second editions, my thanks must first of all go to Dr Narayani Gupta and Dr Yunus Jaffery for their continued willingness to help in any way they could to keep me in touch with new publications related to Delhi and changes in the old city itself.

In the first edition we were indebted to Ramji Narayan for his skilful scrutiny of Red Fort material, Ranjan Monga for help with Old Delhi's commercial life and the late Nigel Hankin for sharing his knowledge of Delhi unrivalled within the British community. Dr John Mitchener wrote the succinct background notes on Hinduism and Rosie and Dilip Singh gave advice on gurdwaras.

In the second edition, I was indebted to the Right Honourable Vijay Goel, who was the MP for Old Delhi at the time, and Mr Mirza Farid Beg for information on Old Delhi's havelis. My thanks also went out to my 'walk-testers', Ben and Sam Spiller and Carol Hogg, for testing the walks during the hot months of July and August 2002 when the pool at Maidens was a tempting alternative.

For this third edition I would particularly like to thank Swapna Liddle for coming to Old Delhi to share her knowledge of the old city as a fellow walker, and Dr Parvez Ahmed Khan, Warden of M M Begg Hostel, The Anglo Arabic Senior Secondary School, for advice on gaining entry to the Madrasa and Tomb of Ghazi-uddin. I very much appreciated the time Dr Aslam Parvaiz,

Principal of Zakir Husain College (Delhi University) spent with me explaining the principles behind Delhi College, the way the culture of Delhi has changed over the last twenty years, and how life in the old city has become more stressful for its residents. I'd also like to thank Simin Jaffry for her contribution to information about the Kasturba Gandhi Hospital.

Finally, my deepest gratitude goes to my husband David Spiller for coming out to Delhi to do what he did for the first edition—test each walk. He did the job most thoroughly and I am extremely grateful. He also proof read the drafts and added dozens of commas I'd missed! Thanks David, you're a star! I'd also like to thank Janice Young, Pamela Timms, and James Tynte-Irvine for supplementing David's checks.

Hotel Broadway provided personal support during the two months I spent in Old Delhi. The reception staff went out of their way to be helpful. Thank you Broadway.